Macdonald Educational

Hannibal

This book is dedicated to H. Russell
Robinson, M.A., F.S.A., of the New
Armouries, Tower of London, who died on
the 15th of January, 1978, in thanks for
his encouragement and help with this
series of books.

The author wishes to thank the following
for their advice:
Professor Howard H. Scullard
Dr Graham Ritchie
Dr Brian Dobson of Durham University
Dr Henry Hurst of the British Carthage
Expedition
Dr Ulrich Schaaff of the Römisch
Germanisches Zentralmuseum, Mainz,
Germany
Dr Ian Stead, British Museum
The Greek and Roman Department of the
British Museum

First published 1978
Macdonald Educational
Holywell House
Worship Street
London EC2A 2EN

ISBN 0 356 05905 7

© Macdonald Educational Limited
1978

Made and printed by
Morrison and Gibb Ltd
London and Edinburgh

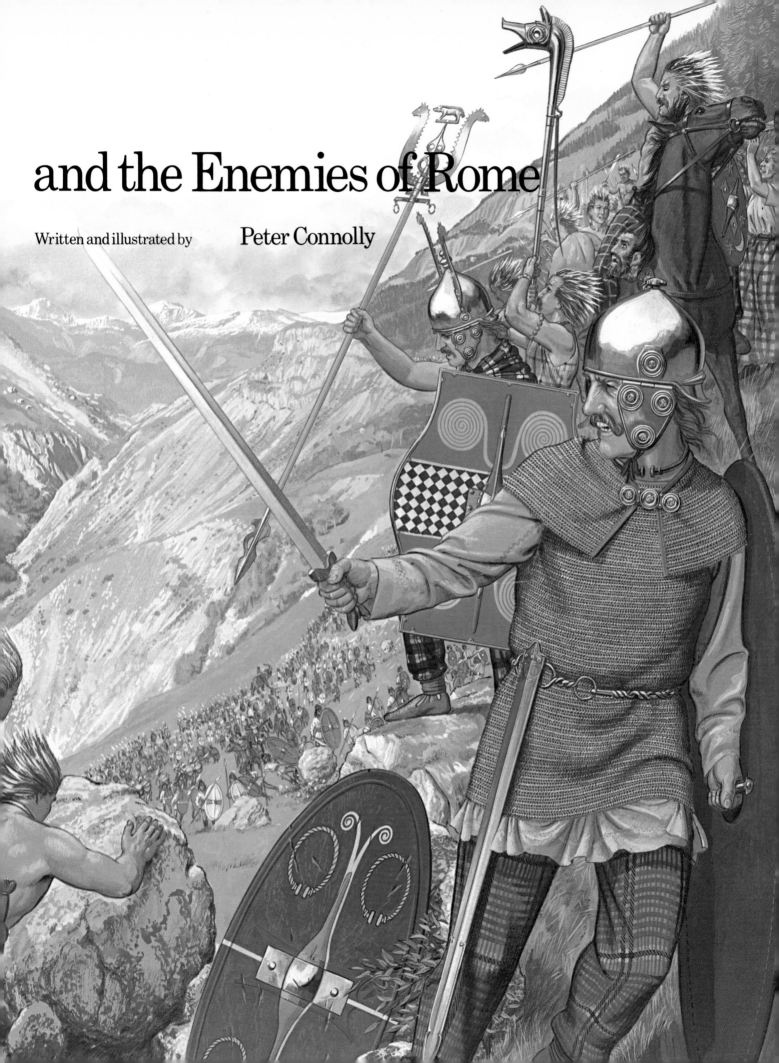

and the Enemies of Rome

Written and illustrated by Peter Connolly

Hannibal

In 218 B.C., Hannibal Barca, a young Carthaginian general, led an army from southern Spain, across the Pyrenees, through France and over the Alps into northern Italy. This epic journey through hostile country has fired everyone's imagination for more than two thousand years. Why did Hannibal do it?

In the previous hundred years Rome had emerged as master of Italy. She had conquered the Etruscans, Samnites and Celts, and had driven the Carthaginians from Western Sicily, their stronghold for centuries.

Hannibal's dream was to raise the banner of revolt in Italy and to unite all Rome's enemies. With a veteran army of mercenaries raised in Spain he descended on northern Italy, and almost succeeded. In three resounding victories he killed about 100,000 Roman soldiers. When Rome overcame Hannibal all of the Mediterranean was hers.

The first part of this book deals with the struggle for the mastery of central Italy, in the 6th-4th centuries B.C. It examines the military systems, armour and weapons of the Etruscans, Samnites and other native people of Italy. It traces the development of the Roman military system, first when Rome was only an Etruscan frontier town, later when she was a member of the Latin League. In the middle of the 4th century B.C. Rome became master of the Latin League and the histories of Italy and Rome became one.

The second part deals with the Carthaginians and their allies. It examines the Carthaginian navy, its ships and harbours. It considers its army, its generals and the revolutionary tactics of Hannibal, probably the greatest military tactician of all. The Carthaginian mercenary troops are also studied: the Numidians, Spaniards and Celts. A quarter of the book is devoted to the Celts. These proud warriors were Rome's bitterest and longest-standing enemies. For 500 years they fought the Romans in Italy, France and Britain until their warrior class was virtually exterminated.

and the Enemies of Rome

CONTENTS

The Etruscans and Samnites

During the sixth century B.C. the Etruscans established a formidable empire in Italy stretching from the Po valley in the north to Campania in the south. These mysterious people rise out of the mists of prehistory. Unfortunately we know of them only from their enemies, the Greeks and the Romans. Their writing has still not been fully translated.

At the end of the sixth century the Latins rebelled and expelled the Etruscans. Rome, which under an Etruscan overlord had been the centre of Etruscan power in Latium, was compelled to fight for her very existence. Over the following two hundred years, Rome took on all-comers and finally, after overcoming the Latins, Etruscans and Samnites, emerged as master of central Italy.

The main source of our knowledge of this period is the Roman historian Titus Livius. Although Livy is a great writer he is a poor historian. As an aristocrat and patriot he throws the blame for many of Rome's mistakes on the lower classes who were struggling for recognition. He also regularly covers up anything that is unfavourable to Rome. He freely uses terms belonging to later periods of history, in spite of their inaccuracy. Worst of all, he often gives accounts that he must know are false.

Dionysius of Halicarnassus has left us a very full account of the early history of Rome. Although he transmits most of the same legends as Livy his account seems to be a little more reliable on military matters. Unfortunately his history is mostly lost after the early fifth century. For the period from 475-265 B.C. we are almost entirely at the mercy of Livy. The archaeological record, however, is excellent, and helps us to draw a clearer picture of this time.

◀ *Lars Porsena, the Etruscan king of Clusium (Chiusi), directs his troops to attack Rome which lies across the river Tiber. The Etruscans are armed with round hoplite shields. The others are mercenaries and Etruscan allies from central and northern Italy.*

9

The Age of Romulus

Romulus and the villages of Rome

In the mountains to the north of Arezzo rise the rivers Arno and Tiber. The Arno flows into the Tyrrhenian sea near Pisa, and the Tiber, after meandering through the marshy plains of northern Latium, flows out at Ostia. Between these two rivers was Etruria, the homeland of the Etruscans. About 25kms from the sea some low hills rose above the marshes on either side of the Tiber. These hills formed the only approach to the river in its lower reaches. Here, in the 8th century B.C. villages sprang up on the hills on the south bank to control the

▲ A group of 8th-century 'Villanovan' warriors. This is the sort of armour that Romulus might have worn. Only the wealthiest could afford helmets and breastplates.

The warrior in the age of Romulus

The communities established on the hills at Rome in the 8th century B.C. were very much the same as those of Etruria. Armour, probably worn only by the wealthiest few, was of beaten bronze decorated with embossing. This armour consisted of a helmet and a cuirass which was usually only a small breastplate. Shields varied from large body shields to smaller round types.

Warriors fought on foot with spears, javelins, swords, daggers and axes. Chariots do not seem to have been in use in the 8th century, although the famous chariot from the Regolini-Galassi tomb at Caere shows that they were a century later. Fighting was probably done in some loose form of phalanx possibly organized by centuries.

Swords

Swords vary from long slashing weapons to short stabbing ones. These swords are of central European type. The commonest form is the antennae sword with its bronze handle with spiral horns (right, **1, 2, 3**). These swords are almost always bronze although a few iron examples do exist. Some swords are plain slashing types with a slightly curved sabre-like blade (**3**). Others have leaf-shaped blades for cutting and thrusting (**1**), while others have long points for thrusting only. The length of blade varies from 33-55cm.

Daggers

Daggers are mainly of the types (**8**) and (**9**) right. Blades are usually bronze but iron examples such as (**8**) have been found. Blades are sometimes triangular, (**9**), and sometimes leaf-shaped. The commonest type has straight sides which curve in towards the bottom to form a long narrow point. Blade lengths vary from 25-41cm. Handles are made of wood, bone or even stone but never of bronze.

traffic crossing the river. The most important of these villages was the one on the Palatine Hill. According to legend this village was established by Romulus and was called Rome after him. King Romulus took the title of *Pontifex Maximus* (bridge-builder-in-chief). This title remained as the name of Rome's chief priest and is borne by the Pope to this day.

In Etruria there were many villages just like these. In these villages a high iron age culture developed (known to the archaeologists as Villanovan) foreshadowing the great Etruscan culture of the following centuries.

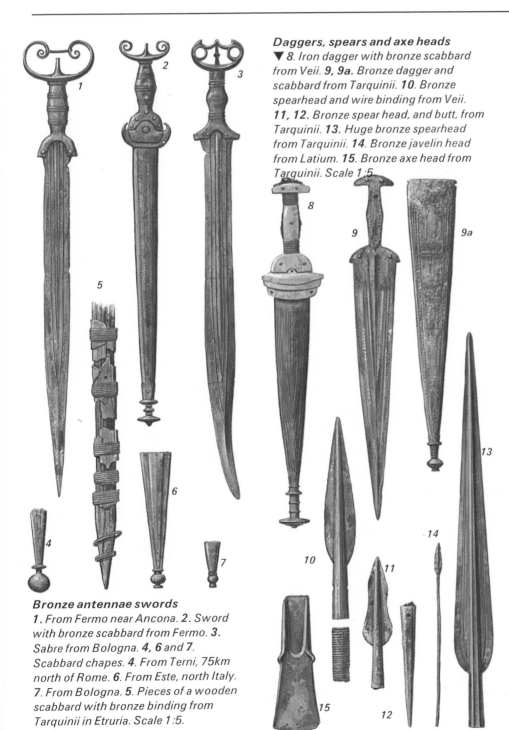

Daggers, spears and axe heads
▼ 8. Iron dagger with bronze scabbard from Veii. 9, 9a. Bronze dagger and scabbard from Tarquinii. 10. Bronze spearhead and wire binding from Veii. 11, 12. Bronze spear head, and butt, from Tarquinii. 13. Huge bronze spearhead from Tarquinii. 14. Bronze javelin head from Latium. 15. Bronze axe head from Tarquinii. Scale 1:5

Bronze antennae swords
1. From Fermo near Ancona. 2. Sword with bronze scabbard from Fermo. 3. Sabre from Bologna. 4, 6 and 7. Scabbard chapes. 4. From Terni, 75km north of Rome. 6. From Este, north Italy. 7. From Bologna. 5. Pieces of a wooden scabbard with bronze binding from Tarquinii in Etruria. Scale 1:5.

Scabbards
Scabbards for the shorter swords are sometimes made of bronze (2). On long swords usually only the bronze chape (metal tip) survives (4, 6, 7). The rest was probably made of wood, perhaps covered with leather. Fragments of wooden scabbards bound with bronze wire have been found (5). Dagger scabbards are usually of beaten bronze with a cast bronze chape. They are often elaborately engraved. The top of the scabbard of swords and daggers is always made separately and is very often missing. This is because it was usually made of a perishable material: (8) is made of bone. The strap (baldric) was attached to this.

Spears and javelins
Bronze spear heads and butts have been found in position in graves so that we know the length of these weapons: from 1·45m-1·85m. The size of spear heads varies vastly from the huge example (13), which is 52cm long, to tiny javelin heads. The bronze javelin head (14) with its long thin shaft is an antecedent of the later Roman heavy javelin (*pilum*). Bronze weapons were cast from molten metal. Iron weapons were beaten into shape as it was impossible to obtain sufficient temperature to cast iron. In fact beaten weapons are far more efficient than cast ones.

The Greek phalanx
The Greek phalanx was introduced into Italy in the seventh century B.C. It was a close formation of spearmen drawn up in a long line several ranks deep. Each soldier was armed with a round shield which protected him and the unguarded side of the man on his left. In this formation the whole army acted as one unit. It needed no standards, as these were used only to keep together small independent units which might otherwise have scattered.

Armour in the Age of Romulus

The coming of the Etruscans

To the north of the Tiber the Villanovan civilization flourished. A powerful ruling class arose. They united groups of villages to form powerful city states. These rulers were the Etruscans. They were great seafarers and may well have come to Italy by sea from the east. Their sea captains soon established a trading empire in the western Mediterranean. But there were other contenders for this trade: the Phoenicians operating from Carthage on the north coast of Africa, and the Greeks who had colonized the southern coasts of Italy and eastern Sicily. One

▲ *4. Round capped helmet with cast bronze crest holder. Origin unknown. Karlsruhe Museum, Germany.*
5. Round capped helmet with bronze crest tube. From Fermo near Ancona.

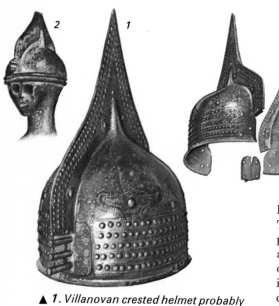

▲ *1. Villanovan crested helmet probably from southern Etruria. Now in the British Museum. 2. Head of a figurine from Bologna showing how the helmet was worn. 3. Exploded drawing of the helmet to show its construction.*

Helmets

The most characteristic helmet of this period was the bronze crested type (see above, 1). This was an exaggerated form of a central European type. It was made in two parts joined along the edge of the crest. The lower edges at the front and back joined by two rectangular plates which were riveted on (see exploded drawing, 3). These helmets, like all armour of this period, are decorated with bosses. The three long spikes at front and back were purely decorative and had no function. The way this type of helmet was worn is clearly shown on a figurine from northern Italy (2).

The commonest form of helmet was the round capped type. Some of these have cast bronze crest holders which are hollowed out to take the crest pin (4). One example from Fermo near Ancona has a crest tube made of bronze plate (5).

Body armour

The commonest form of body armour was the small square bronze breast and back plates (7, 8). Several of these have been found. They vary from 15-22cm in depth. Hundreds of round breast plates have been found (see p.16).

The elaborate poncho type armour (6) was discovered at Narce in Etruria: it dates from about 700 B.C. A few belt hooks and plates have been found (9, 10).

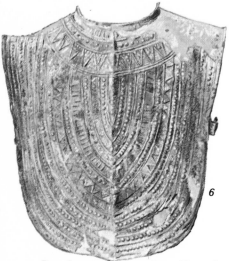

▲ *Poncho type cuirass from Narce in Etruria. A similar cuirass made of gold was found in the Regolini-Galassi tomb at Caere.*

▲ *7 and 8. Bronze beast plates. 7. From Tarquinii. 8. From Latium. 9. Bronze belt clasp from Terni. 10. Pierced bronze belt plate from Altri.*
All scale 1:5.

such colony was at Cumae just west of Naples. These Greeks began interfering with Etruscan trade with the east. This interference developed into a bitter feud between the two nations.

About 616 B.C. the Etruscans forced their way across the Tiber, captured the Roman villages and established a land route south through Latium. The Etruscan armies pressed on southwards into Campania by-passing Cumae. They captured several of the coastal towns including Pompeii and Sorrento and established a large military colony at Capua just south of the Volturno river.

Ceremonial shields

Many round shields have been found, all dating to the later Villanovan period. These are made of embossed bronze and vary in width from 50cm-1m. These shields do not have a wooden core as one would expect. The handgrip and strap fasteners are fixed directly onto the inside of the bronze. Sometimes they have been worked so thin that the bronze has 'holed' during construction. Similar shields have been found at the Greek sanctuary at Olympia. These shields are clearly made for ceremonial purposes: they would be absolutely useless in battle. However, they were based on functional examples, none of which have been found.

Battle shields

Real shields were probably made of wood or wicker with rawhide facing. Rome's treaty with the Gabini was inscribed on a wooden shield covered with oxhide. These shields may have been decorated with metal studs. In fact all the armour of this period may have developed from hide or wicker covered with bronze studs, which would explain the embossing.

The scutum

The oval body shield (*scutum*) was almost certainly in use. (See the picture on p.10.) These shields had the central handgrip common to all shields before the introduction of the hoplite shield in the 7th century B.C.

▲ Villanovan embossed bronze shield from Bisenzio near Florence. Scale 1:6. *1. The front of the shield showing the round central boss with three rivets above and below it. These were to fasten on the handgrip. 2. The back of the shield showing the handgrip. The five hanging attachments were probably for carrying-straps similar to Greek shields. 3. Section of the shield showing wood-filled handle. 4. Detail of the handle.*

Etruscan Military Organization

Etruscan kings at Rome

An Etruscan military overlord was established at Rome. He grouped the villages together into a town as had been done in Etruria. For the next hundred years under its three Etruscan kings Rome flourished and became the chief city in Latium.

The Etruscans reached the summit of their power when they formed an alliance with the Carthaginians against their common enemy, the Greeks, whom they expelled from their colony at Alalia in Corsica after a sea battle in 535 B.C.

But the Etruscan age of glory was short lived.

The Etruscan armies

Each Etruscan city had its own army. Although these cities were united by a league they seldom operated together which was their great weakness. Some cities might combine on a particular expedition and the conquest of the south must have been just such a venture. However, like the Greek city states, they spent most of their energy fighting each other.

In the 7th century B.C. the Etruscans adopted the Greek method of fighting and organized their armies into phalanxes. Like the later Romans the Etruscans relied heavily on troops from peoples either conquered by or in alliance with them.

In the Roman army of this period we are probably seeing a typical Etruscan army. Under the first Etruscan king, Tarquinius Priscus, the army was divided into three separate groups: Etruscans, who formed a phalanx, and Romans and Latins, who fought in their freer native style.

The reforms of Servius Tullius

Servius Tullius, the second Etruscan king, tried to integrate the population by organising the army according to wealth and not race. He divided the whole population into six classes. The first, or richest class, he formed into 80 units (centuries). The Etruscans must still have formed the majority of this class. These made up the phalanx. The second class formed 20 centuries and likewise the third and fourth classes. These were all spearmen. The fifth class formed 30 centuries who were slingers. The sixth, or poorest, performed no military duties.

When an army was needed each of these centuries provided men in proportion to the total required, i.e. if an army of 10,000 was needed each century would provide about 60 men. Attached to the army were two centuries of horn and trumpet blowers and two centuries of armourers and engineers (fabri). The army was divided in half by age. The veterans served as home guard and the youngsters went on campaign.

▲ Warriors with round, oval and four-sided shields from the Certosa Situla.

▼ Early representations of the scutum. 1. From Vetulonia. 2. From Este. 3. A spined boss from Malpasso.

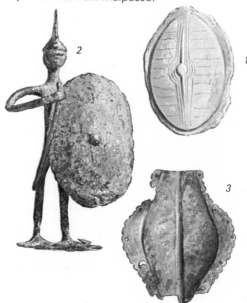

14

Although they had isolated Cumae by their thrust southwards into Campania they failed to bring the Greek city to its knees. In fact in 524 B.C. they suffered a serious defeat on land at the hands of the Cumaeans. Fourteen years later, probably egged on by the Cumaeans, the Latins rebelled, and Rome expelled her Etruscan ruler Tarquin the Proud. This revolt spelt disaster for the Etruscans as the Romans now closed the river crossing to them.

Tarquin fled to Tuscany and from here plotted his return to power. He called upon the Etruscan cities which were close to Rome to support him. Tarquinii and Veii answered the call and, with an army supplied by these two towns, Tarquin marched on Rome. The Latins advanced to meet him. The battle was indecisive but the very fact that they had survived was sufficient for the Romans to celebrate a triumph.

Lars Porsena, king of Clusium (Chiusi), who realized that control of Rome was essential now entered the fray. Collecting together a large army of Etruscans, allies and mercenaries he made a lightning advance southwards on Rome hoping he could take the city by surprise.

Armament

The soldiers of the phalanx were armed in Greek fashion with round Argive shield, bronze cuirass, greaves, helmet, spear and sword. The phalanx was backed up by three lines of troops who were armed in Italian fashion with a large body shield. The first line, from the second class, were armed with spear, sword, helmet and greaves. The next line had only a spear, sword and helmet: the last line a spear and javelin but no armour.

After the Etruscans

When the Etruscan kings were driven out of Rome a large proportion of the first class must have gone with them. This would account for Rome's much reduced military capability. Livy states that the round shield continued in use until the introduction of pay at the end of the 5th century. But it could have been abandoned earlier when Rome was forced to join the Latin League and conform to its military organisation.

The Italian body shield

Livy refers to the shield used by classes 2-4 as a *scutum*. This was the name given to the large oval shield used by the legionaries of the later republic. However Dionysius and Diodorus describe it as "four-sided". Here archaeology has come to our aid. Bologna was an Etruscan frontier town situated in an almost identical position to Rome but on the northern frontier. The Certosa *Situla*, a bronze bucket of c. 500 B.C., was found here. This bucket has warrior figures embossed on it. They are carrying round hoplite shields, oval shields and four-sided shields.

This four-sided shield was probably only a variation of the oval *scutum* which certainly existed in central Italy at this time. The 7th century sculpture from Etruria and the bronze boss from the central highlands (see left) prove that the traditional oval *scutum* with spined boss was also in use from the earliest times.

▲ *A horn-blower from N. Italy.*

▼ *The Etrusco-Roman field army composed of 40 centuries of hoplites, 10 centuries of medium and 10 centuries of light-armed spearmen, 10 centuries of skirmishers and 15 centuries of slingers. The size of the centuries depended on the number of troops needed.*

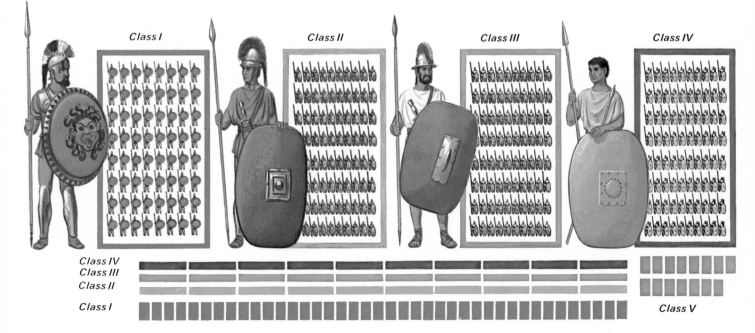

Etruscan Armour and Weapons

Etruscan armour

The tactics and armour of the Greek phalanx were adopted by the Etruscans in the 7th century B.C. Although Greek helmets and cuirasses were widely used, Italian types remained popular. The sculpture above and the tomb painting from Chiusi (below right) show Etruscans in totally Greek attire. The only clue to the Italian origin of the Chiusi warrior are the feathers on his helmet. The the reconstructed grave group seen below shows typically mixed equipment: Greek shield, Italian helmet and Graeco-Etruscan greaves.

Body armour

Although Greek cuirasses were widely used, many examples of circular breast plates have been found. The dating of these discs is very difficult as we are not sure where they were found. The use of this type of armour was widespread. The discs have been found in Spain and central Europe. They are even shown on Assyrian bas-reliefs.

Helmets

The most common form of helmet in use in this period was the Negau type (right, **2**) called after a Yugoslavian village where a large number were found.

The earliest datable example of this type of helmet is the one on the left (c.525 B.C.). The type remained in use unchanged right down to the 4th and possibly the 3rd century B.C. These helmets have a flat ring with stitching holes attached to the inside of the rim. This held a lining which kept the helmet well up on the head.

Although this type of helmet normally had a crest which followed the ridge from front to back, several examples have been found with attachments for a transverse crest (see right, **2**). This type of crest was worn by Roman centurions. This could point to an Etruscan origin for the famed Roman centurionate.

Leg guards

Several examples of Greek style greaves have been found in Italy. The commonest form is based on a Greek 6th century style (**5-7** above). This type has no shaping for the knee, a common feature of Greek greaves. The greaves remained in use as long as the Negau helmet and are often found with them.

Thigh, ankle and foot guards which were in use in Greece in the 6th century were very popular for a much longer period in Etruria. Arm guards were also popular.

▲ Sculpture of Etruscan warriors from Falerii Veteres. They are wearing complete Greek panoply: helmet, greaves, thigh guards and linen cuirass.

Far left: typical Etruscan armour and weapons. The armour is reconstructed from the mixed panoply found in the Tomb of the Warrior at Vulci c. 525 B.C. It consists of a Greek hoplite shield, Graeco-Etruscan greaves and Italian helmet.

▼ Helmets from Etruscan graves. **1.** Greek 'Chalcidian' type. **2.** Italian 'Negau' type. **3.** Inside the rim of (2) showing band for stitching in lining.

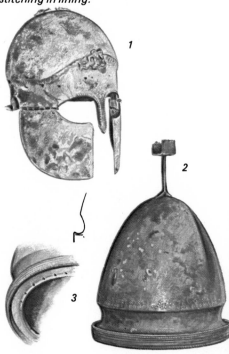

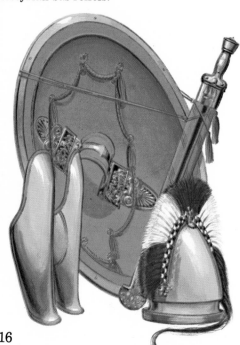

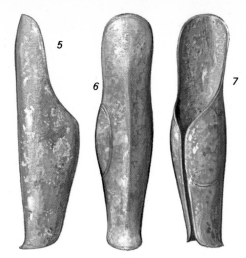

Etruscan weapons

▲ 5, 6 and 7. Side, front and back of an Etruscan greave from the Tomb of the Warrior at Vulci. This type remained unchanged for more than 200 years.

1. Spear head. 2. Javelin head. 3. Greek type of sword from Etruscan Alalia in Corsica. 4 and 5. Handle and scabbard chape from similar swords. 6. Pilum. 7. Typical belt clasp. 8, 9, 10. Development of the curved sword. 8. Early Italian (bronze). 9. Etruscan. 10. Spanish.

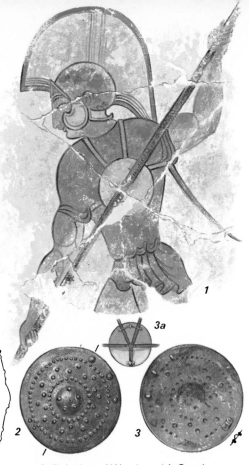

▲ 1. Painting of Warrior with Greek helmet and Etruscan round breastplate from Ceri. 2 and 3. Front and back of round breastplate. 3a. Back of plate showing harnessing.

▼ 4. Warrior with complete Greek panoply but with Italian-style feathers on his helmet. From Chiusi (Clusium).

The shield

The hoplite shield had been generally adopted in Etruria in the 7th century. Occasional representations of the oval shield (the forerunner of the Roman *scutum* and the Celtic shield) have been found (see p.15). This body shield was probably the original shield of the Italians and was never really used by the Etruscans, only by Italians serving with the Etruscan army. The example from Vetulonia (see p.14) probably comes from the period before absolute Etruscan domination of the area. The boss from a spined shield of this type (also shown on p.14) comes from near Gualdo Tadino beyond the eastern border of Etruria.

Weapons

During this period the Etruscans adopted the Greek sword (see 3 in the box). The curved sword (9 right) was very popular in Greece and Spain in the 6th-3rd centuries: it seems to have originated in Etruria, where examples have been found dating back to the 7th century. The bronze sabre from Este in northern Italy (8) may be the forerunner of this weapon, and testify to its Italian origin.

The Etruscan and early Greek weapons were long chopping swords. The later Macedonian and Spanish weapons (10) were pointed cut and thrust swords. A variety of spearheads have been found in Etruria. The long Villanovan type was still very popular during this period. The socketed head of a long javelin *(pilum)* was found in a 5th century grave at Vulci (6).

Allies and Enemies: The Hill Peoples

Horatius and the bridge

The Romans realized that the attack must come and made desperate preparations. A fort was established on the Janiculum, a hill on the Etruscan side of the river which covered the approach to the bridge, and the Romans armed themselves to do or die.

In spite of their preparations, the Romans were caught off-guard. The Etruscans stormed the Janiculum and advanced on the bridge. In panic the Romans turned and ran. Livy tells how Horatius and his two companions, who, ironically, have Etruscan names, bravely held back the enemy while their

▲ A warrior from the hills. This type of armour and weapons would have been used by the Hernici, Aequi and Volsci. He wears a 'pot' helmet, neck-guard and a circular breastplate and backplate. He carries two throwable spears and a Greek-type sword. **1** and **2** show the front and back of a breastplate and backplate from Alfedena, scale 1:8. **3**. Reconstruction of a two-disc cuirass showing harnessing.

The early hill peoples

During the early years of the 5th century Rome came into violent contact with the hill peoples of central Italy: the Aequi, Hernici and Volsci. These are just three of the many tribes who, with the Samnites and Sabines, occupied the Apennine hills which run from north to south of Italy.

Excavations at Alfedena on the northern border of Samnium, and at Campovalano di Campli, near Teramo, have produced a wealth of arms and armour. These finds, when compared to the famous warrior statue found at Capestrano about 30km east of L'Aquila, enable us to draw up an accurate picture of a hill people's warrior.

▲ The warrior of Capestrano showing the disc breastplate and sword. The helmet with its vast brim is probably grossly exaggerated. Below: back of the same figure.

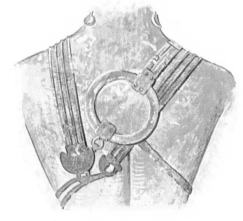

18

companions chopped down the bridge. Some Roman historians do admit the Etruscans recaptured Rome.

The Etruscan army marched on into Latium and advanced on Aricia, the centre of the Latin resistance. The Greeks from Cumae marched north to meet them. Caught between the Latins and the Greeks, Lars Porsena's army was cut to pieces and the Etruscan king was forced to flee to Etruria.

With their land route cut the Etruscans were forced to try to maintain contact with their colonies by sea. In 474 B.C. they were defeated by the Greeks in a sea battle off Cumae and the towns of Campania were completely cut off. But fate had a trick to play: only 50 years later both Etruscan Capua and Greek Cumae were captured by the Samnites.

Meanwhile, Rome, which had controlled Latium under her Etruscan kings, was trying desperately to hold on to her position. Ultimately she was forced to sign a treaty of alliance with the other Latin towns as equal partners. The next 80 years were spent fighting for her very existence against the eastern hill peoples, the Aequi, Hernici and Volsci who were being forced down into the plains of Latium by the expansion of the Samnites.

The breastplate

The Capestrano warrior (left, **4**, **5**) has a round breastplate and backplate held in place by a hinged metal strap which passes over his right shoulder. Two fabric or leather straps pass under the arms and hold the two plates in place over his heart. Many of these plates have been found (left, **1**, **2**). They are closely related to the Etruscan discs. Besides examples from Alfedena and Campovalano they have also been found as far afield as Caserta in Campania and the Etruscan town of Alalia in Corsica. The plates are made of bronze with an iron backing. These plates are joined by a hinged shoulder strap, also bronze with iron backing.

Many broad rimmed helmets have been found but none with a rim as broad as that worn by the Capestrano warrior. A helmet of unknown origin at the Vatican has a very broad brim and this may very well be the type shown (see p.20, **3**).

Examples of greaves, neck guards and upper and lower arm guards have also been found (below **2-5**).

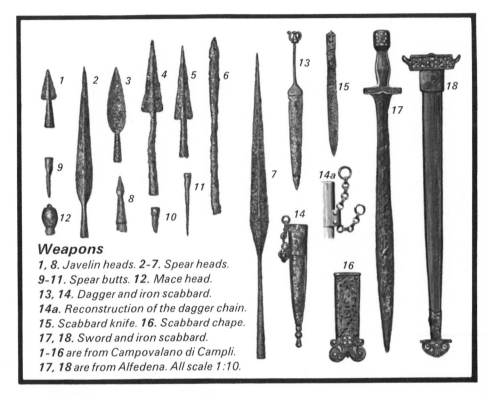

Weapons
1, 8. Javelin heads. 2-7. Spear heads.
9-11. Spear butts. 12. Mace head.
13, 14. Dagger and iron scabbard.
14a. Reconstruction of the dagger chain.
15. Scabbard knife. 16. Scabbard chape.
17, 18. Sword and iron scabbard.
1-16 are from Campovalano di Campli.
17, 18 are from Alfedena. All scale 1:10.

1. Decorated breastplate from near Ancona. 2. Greave. 3. Throat guard.
4. Upper arm guard. 5. Lower arm guard.
2. From Campovalano. 3,4,5. From Alfedena.

Weapons

Many swords of Greek type have been found. One is almost identical to the Capestrano warrior's (above, **17-18**). A small knife is often found resting on the sword, as with the Capestrano warrior (**15**). Some daggers have been found. The antennae-like projections on the handles indicate central European origin (**13**).

On either side of the Capestrano warrior is a javelin with a throwing loop.

Dozens of examples of spear and javelin heads and butts have been found. They vary from the leaf-shaped Greek type (**3**), to diamond shape (**7**) and the unique triangular blades (**4**, **5**) found all along the Adriatic side of Italy. Several spears have been found in place in the graves, varying in length from 1·5m-2·2m.

19

Allies and Enemies: Northern Peoples

Trouble from the north

By the end of the sixth century B.C. the situation in the south had become impossible and the Etruscans had to find a new outlet for their trade with the east. Around 500 B.C. an Etruscan colony was established at Bologna in the Po valley and a route opened up to Spina, a port at the head of the Adriatic. But, like the route to the south, this route was doomed.

For some time the Celts of central Europe had been forcing their way over the Alps and settling in the Po valley. This migration built up as the 5th century went on. By the end of the century the Etruscans

The Northern Peoples

During the 6th and 5th centuries B.C. another culture flourished just south of the Alps. This included the whole area of the Po valley and north-western Yugoslavia. These people had a unique art-form known to archaeologists as *situla* art. These *situlae* are bronze buckets which are often elaborately decorated with embossed figures. Often they show warriors and chariots. These representations, coupled with the weapons and armour that have been found, enable us to build up a pretty accurate picture of the north Italian warrior. Shields of all shapes and sizes are shown on these *situlae*, from round hoplite shields to oval and rectangular body shields. The shield boss (left, **3**) is from Yugoslavia. This is from a body shield. Its sections show that it was from a convex shield. Shields of this type are often shown in Italian early Roman art.

1, 2. Warriors shown on situlae: *2 may be an early Celt. 3. Iron shield boss from Yugoslavia. 4. Chariots shown on a* situla *from Vače in Yugoslavia.*

were under pressure from both north and south. Rome, which had gradually established itself as head of the Latin League, launched an all-out attack on the Etruscan town of Veii, which was captured in 396 B.C. A few years later the Celts burst into Etruria and advanced on Rome. They crushed the legions who were sent to oppose them, and sacked the City on the hills.

Rome recovered, but the days of Etruscan glory were over. The colony at Bologna held on for a few more years but by 350 B.C. it was in Celtic hands.

Rome had suffered a temporary set-back but by 351 B.C. she felt strong enough to launch a double offensive against Tarquinii and Falerii in southern Etruria. Three years later she entered a war to the death with her most implacable enemy of the early years, the Volsci. One question still remained to be solved: who governed Latium, Rome, or the military confederation of Latin towns which was the Latin League in the 5th-4th centuries B.C.? In 340 B.C. the final struggle began. After a bitter war that lasted three years Rome emerged as undisputed master. All the tribes of western Italy between the Tiber and Campania were under Roman control.

Sixth century Italian pot helmets

1. Early helmet. 2. Four-piece helmet. 2a. Exploded view of 2. 2b. Similar helmet from a situla. 3. Broad-brimmed helmet. 4. Half breed Negau/pot helmet. 5. Helmet with lead-filled bosses. 5a, 5b. Boss showing lead filling. 6. Helmet made of discs and studs over a wicker frame. 6a. Similar helmet from the Certosa situla. 6b. Top knot of a disc and stud helmet. 6c. Fragment of wicker frame. 7. Conical helmet. 7a. Conical helmet from a situla.

Helmets

The predominant type then was the pot helmet. The earliest form (1) is a simple round cap turned out at the brim. A similar helmet was found at Rome. This type often has small knobs riveted on. Number 2 is a type common to northern Italy and Yugoslavia. It is made of four pieces riveted together. Type (3) is unusual, for only two examples have been found. It is interesting because of its broad brim, the nearest yet found to the immense brim of the Capestrano statue. Type (4) is common around the northern Adriatic. Type (5) is found only in the area between Ancona and Bari on the Adriatic coast. About ten examples of type (5) exist. All have two bronze bosses riveted to the side. These bosses are filled with lead and backed with an iron disc. The Negau type (p.17) was obviously related to this group of helmets.

The *situla* from Certosa (Bologna) shows a peculiar helmet made up of bosses or discs (6a). Examples of this type have been found in Yugoslavia (6). They are made of á wicker base like a basket (6c) covered with bronze discs. The gaps are filled with bronze studs. Cuirasses made of bronze studs have also been found. The last type (7) is not very common. All these helmets are held on by chin straps and have no cheek-pieces. Types (1-5) had crests.

Greaves

Greaves were sometimes worn: a pair was found in the famous warrior grave at Sesto Calende, north of Milan, with a helmet of type (2) and the iron rim of a chariot wheel. Similar burials have been found around Ancona.

Weapons

The *situlae* show warriors armed with spears, javelins, swords and axes. Examples of all these have been found.

The Samnites 450-250 B.C.

First blood

The war with the Volsci had brought Rome face to face with the Samnites. They were the largest group of native Italian people and occupied the hills of central southern Italy. Rome had signed a treaty with them in 354 B.C. to enlist their aid against their mutual enemy, the Volsci. In 343 B.C. hostilities broke out that were to last for 50 years.

The Samnites, finding that the war had suddenly got out of hand, lost interest in it and after three years of indecisive skirmishing, backed off. For 15 years Romans and Samnites eyed each other suspici-

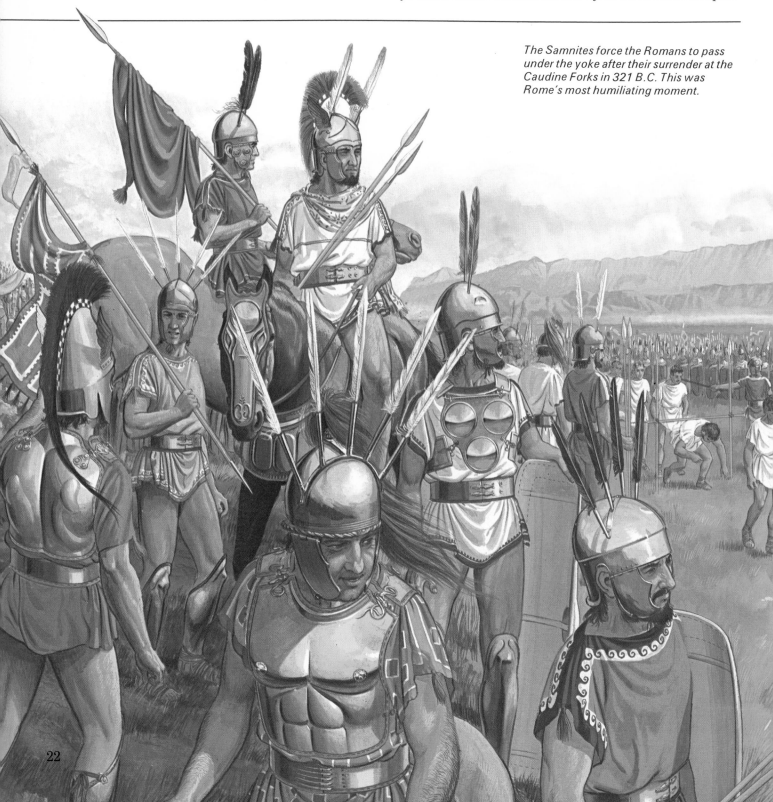

The Samnites force the Romans to pass under the yoke after their surrender at the Caudine Forks in 321 B.C. This was Rome's most humiliating moment.

ously. Both knew that a conflict must come.

The point of contact was along the Liris river. The Romans occupied the western and the Samnites the eastern bank. In 328 B.C. the Romans established a colony at Fregellae on the Samnite side of the river. In response the Samnites engineered a *coup* at Naples and detached the town from its Roman alliance. Rome had the excuse she needed and declared war.

The first years of this war were again characterised by inconclusive skirmishes: the Samnites not wishing to take on the Romans in the plains, and the Romans fearful of advancing into the hills.

In 321 B.C. the senate decided to make a thrust into the heart of the Samnite country. For this purpose the two consuls combined their armies at Calatia in northern Campania.

The Samnites had elected a general of genius, Gavius Pontius. When he was informed that the legions were gathering at Calatia he guessed where the strike was to come. As the road from Calatia into the Samnite territory leaves the plains it passes through a narrow gap in the hills. This place was known as the Caudine Forks. Here Gavius waited with his army on the hilltops around the road.

The Samnite conquests

The Samnites occupied the central Italian hill country from the river Sangro in the north to the River Ofanto in the south. This was the area known as Samnium and it was with its people that the Romans fought the Samnite wars. However, the area occupied by tribes directly related to the Samnites was far greater. Soon after 500 B.C., following the collapse of Etruscan power in the south, Samnite tribes poured into the coastal plains. In the next century they occupied the whole of southern Italy from Campania to the toe of Italy.

The fall of Capua and Cumae

The Etruscan colony of Capua fell to them in 423 B.C. In 421 B.C. the Greek city of Cumae, which had played such an important part in the defeat of Lars Porsena, was also captured. Apulia on the east coast had similarly been occupied. The Samnites mingled with the local populations and soon produced independent tribes.

The Samnite Federation

The Samnites tried to force their brothers in Campania into the Samnite federation. It was this that probably caused the Romans to intervene in 343 B.C., as such a federation could have proved a great threat to Rome's ambitions.

The Samnite wars

The long war between Rome and the Samnites is divided by the historians into three parts—the first, second and third Samnite wars. Livy's account of the first war is so bad that many historians have been led to believe that no such war took place. It is certain that no gain was made by either side. Although the historical record is bad, the archaeological record is excellent and helps us build up a good picture of the Samnite warrior.

▲ *Coastal Samnite warriors carrying standards: from Paestum in Lucania. This painting is probably early 4th century.*

The Samnite warrior

There are no unquestionable representations of Samnite warriors. The Samnites who migrated to the coast came under the influence of the Greeks and their armour shows Greek influence.

It is impossible to say how similar the hundreds of representations of coastal Samnites are to the true Samnites. The coastal Samnites are almost always shown with the Greek shield. A fragmentary wall painting at Naples shows warriors with large round or oval shields without the out-turned rim of the hoplite shield (see p.25). This could well be the Italian body shield *(scutum)*. Most warriors wear greaves and Attic type helmets with feathers. All wear the broad bronze Samnite belt. Some have triangular breastplates embossed with three discs. The warriors carry spears or javelins but never swords. Horsemen did not wear greaves: they usually wore instead an anklet (see above, and p. 26).

Samnite gladiators

Livy's description of Samnite armour has no relation to archaeological evidence. He probably described the Samnite gladiator of his day, sculptures of which have been found. They carry a shield, clearly the oval *scutum* with the top cut off, implying the Samnites did use the *scutum*.

Samnite tactics

Livy's account cannot be trusted for details of Samnite military practices, but clearly their army was light-armed and fast moving. Several times they outmanoeuvred the Romans. The paintings suggest the javelin was their prime weapon. The wall paintings also show many examples of flag type standards which prove conclusively they did not fight in phalanx.

Samnite Armour and Weapons

The Caudine Forks

The consuls led their army through the gap and into the plain. When they reached the far end they found the road blocked with felled trees and the Samnites occupying the hillsides. In panic the consuls ordered the retreat. The army dashed back towards the entrance, to find it blocked as well.

For several days the Romans tried to fight their way out. At last, faced with starvation, they had to surrender. The Samnite terms were not harsh. They must withdraw from Samnite territory and abandon their colonies along the borders. They must abide by

Body armour

The type of body armour associated with the Samnites is the triple disc cuirass. Several of these have been found. One beautiful example was discovered at Alfedena (**1**, right). The development of this type of cuirass is impossible to trace. They appear on vase paintings in the middle of the 4th century B.C. They must in some way be connected with the single disc breastplates of the 6th century.

The square breast and backplates shown below (**9, 9a**) are in the British Museum. These appear only on the wallpainting from Paestum (see **10**, below and p.23). They are obviously a development of the Villanovan square breastplates (p.12). Polybius, a reliable source on Graeco-Roman affairs, says this type of armour was still in use in the Roman Army in the 2nd century B.C., when he wrote. The anatomical decoration is influenced by the Greek muscled cuirasses. The detail does not relate to the same points on the wearer's body: the broad belt covers the navel. These cuirasses had shoulder plates like the triple-disc cuirass shown above. They also had side plates, usually hinged to the back plate. None of these side or shoulder plates have been recovered. As we do not know exactly where or when these cuirasses were found, so we cannot say how widespread was their use, or give the limits of their dating. The wall painting from Paestum should date to the period of Samnite occupation, 390-273 B.C.

Belts

The broad bronze Samnite belt (**2**) was always worn. Whatever else a Samnite, Campanian, Apulian or Lucanian might wear, he would always have his belt, which was the symbol of his manhood. Many belts survive with a great variety of hooks (**3-7**).

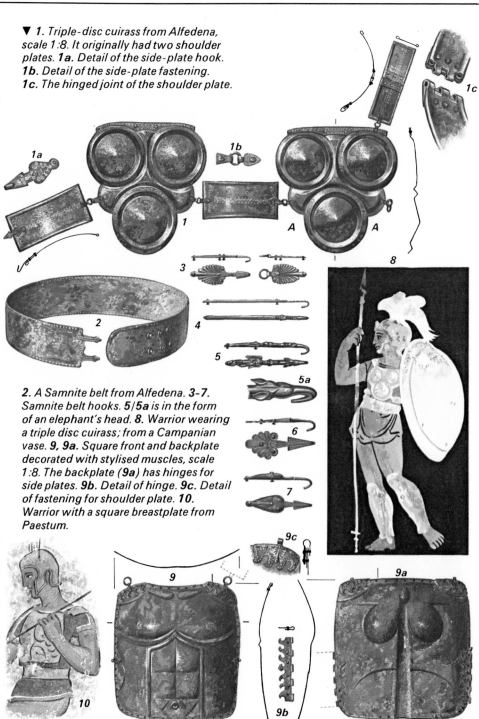

▼ *1. Triple-disc cuirass from Alfedena, scale 1:8. It originally had two shoulder plates. 1a. Detail of the side-plate hook. 1b. Detail of the side-plate fastening. 1c. The hinged joint of the shoulder plate.*

2. A Samnite belt from Alfedena. 3-7. Samnite belt hooks. 5/5a is in the form of an elephant's head. 8. Warrior wearing a triple disc cuirass; from a Campanian vase. 9, 9a. Square front and backplate decorated with stylised muscles, scale 1:8. The backplate (9a) has hinges for side plates. 9b. Detail of hinge. 9c. Detail of fastening for shoulder plate. 10. Warrior with a square breastplate from Paestum.

the treaty signed in 354 B.C. Six hundred knights (*equites*) were to be handed over as hostages. The two consuls signed.

The army was spared but forced to undergo a humilation that they had imposed on so many others before. They were made to leave behind all their belongings and, clad only in a tunic, to "pass under the yoke". This was a frame of two spears stuck in the ground and a third tied across horizontally at a height that compelled one to bend down to pass underneath. This was the symbol of defeat, and kindled in the Roman breast a thirst for revenge.

1. A Samnite Attic helmet in the British Museum. This is the commonest form of Samnite helmet. 2. Samnite Attic helmet in the Castel Sant'Angelo at Rome. 3. Feather holder. 4. Samnite triple disc cheek-piece from Bovianum. 5 and 6. Paintings of Samnite warriors armed with large shields and javelins. 7. Painting of a single-edged slashing sword. 5, 6 and 7. From Naples. 8. A 4th century Samnite warrior.

Helmets and greaves

Many Samnite helmets survive. They are easily recognized by their feather holders. They are usually a modified form of Greek Attic helmet (1, 2). The cheek-piece on the left (4) which comes from Bovianum in central Samnium is identical in design to the triple-disc breastplate. The hinge fitting at the top shows that it comes from an Attic type helmet. The two lobes A-A that protrude from the sides of the cuirass to hold the fastenings for the side plates also appear on the cheek-piece but serve no such useful purpose.

It follows that the cheek-piece was derived from the cuirass and not *vice versa*. This is important, for this type of cheek-piece has always been regarded as of Celtic origin. This cannot be so. It is significant that these lobes were the first characteristic of the triple-disc cheek-pieces that the Celts abandoned (see p.62).

Greaves are shown on the paintings. These are of Greek classical style. Examples have turned up in Lucania and Apulia (see p.27). Some of these greaves have ring attachments for straps. This fashion was adopted by the Romans.

Weapons

A few spear heads have turned up. They are of standard Italian type. Javelins with loops are shown on a painting at Naples (5, 6). There is also a painting at Naples which shows a sword of the single edged slashing type (7) but there are no surviving examples.

Campanians, Lucanians and Apulians

The Samnites march on Rome

The defeated army crept back to Rome in disgrace. The Romans were humiliated and burning for revenge, but for five years they kept the Caudine peace. By 316 B.C. they could hold back no longer. They repudiated the treaty, saying that the consuls had no right to make it and reopened the war on three fronts. One army operated in Campania, one further north in the Liris valley, whilst a third crossed over to the Adriatic coast and marched south to join with the Apulians against the Samnites there.

The Samnites struck like lightning and completely

▶ *1 and 2. A conical and Etrusco-Corinthian helmet from Apulia. 3. An Etrusco-Corinthian helmet from an Etruscan painting. 4. Painting of a horseman from Capua. 5 and 6. A peytral and chamfron. 7. Painting of a horseman from Paestum.*

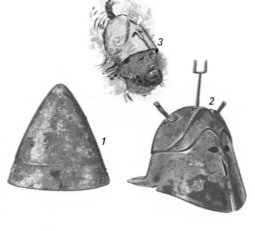

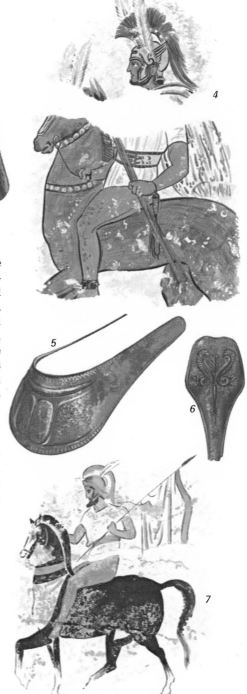

The coastal Samnites

Campania, Lucania and Apulia are the coastal areas surrounding Samnium on the west, south and east. The Samnites expanded here in the 5th-4th century. They came into contact with the Greeks and adopted much of their armour which they altered to suit their own needs.

Campanian cavalry

In the plains of Campania the Samnites developed a formidable cavalry. In the 3rd-2nd century B.C. they formed the backbone of the Roman cavalry. Campanian and northern Lucanian paintings show several horsemen. There was a fine example from Capua (right, 4) which was destroyed in World War II. The horse is wearing a face guard (chamfron) and feathers. On another painting from Paestum the horse is wearing chest armour (7). Examples of both types of armour can be seen at Naples (5, 6).

Armour found in Lucania

Two complete sets of armour have been found in Lucania. One found near Paestum consists of a triple-disc cuirass, helmet and belt (right, 8-10).

A second panoply, now at the Tower of London, consists of a winged helmet, square breast and back-plates, greaves and belt (11-14). The greaves have strap fastenings at the back. The helmet has wings, spring feather holders with snake's head terminals and a raised crest holder. It is very like the helmet of the Capuan horseman (4).

The Apulians

The Apulians came much more under the influence of the Greeks than their kinsmen on Italy's west coast. A beautiful panoply found at Conversano, near Bari, (15-18) consists of a pair of classical Greek greaves, a Greek muscled cuirass, a winged helmet and a Samnite belt. The wave decoration on the cuirass matches the comb on the crest of the helmet, which has feather tubes hidden behind its bronze wings (17a). Fourth century B.C. conical helmets (1) have been found and are often featured on vase paintings.

The so-called Etrusco-Corinthian helmet (2, 3) seems to have originated in Apulia in the 6th century. This type, which was worn like a cap and did not cover the face, remained in use among the Etruscans and Romans until the 1st century B.C.

There was a strong Celtic influence in Apulia. The Celts regularly invaded central Italy in the 4th century B.C., and usually ended up in the cornfields of Apulia. Some may even have settled there. Several mongrel helmets have turned up, and in one Apulian grave a muscled cuirass and Celtic helmet were found.

out-manoeuvred the Romans. Keeping the Roman armies in Apulia and the Liris valley occupied, they brushed aside the Campanian army and advanced northward. The Romans handed over power to a dictator who gathered all available forces and advanced southward. He dispatched half his forces under his deputy (the master of the horse) to cover the coast road (later the Appian Way) while he himself advanced along the Latin Way between the hills.

The Samnite army which had been heading for the Latin Way now changed course, crossed the hills and fell upon the master of the horse near Terracina. The Roman army was annihiliated and its commander killed. Rome's southern allies now rebelled. The Samnites advanced into Latium destroying the crops and ravaging the countryside as far north as Ardea, only 30km from Rome.

In panic the Roman senate recalled part of its forces from the Liris valley. The Samnites there immediately crossed the river and attacked the weakened Roman force. The Romans were on the run. To the north, Rome's central Italian allies wavered. If they defected now, the Roman army in Apulia would be cut off.

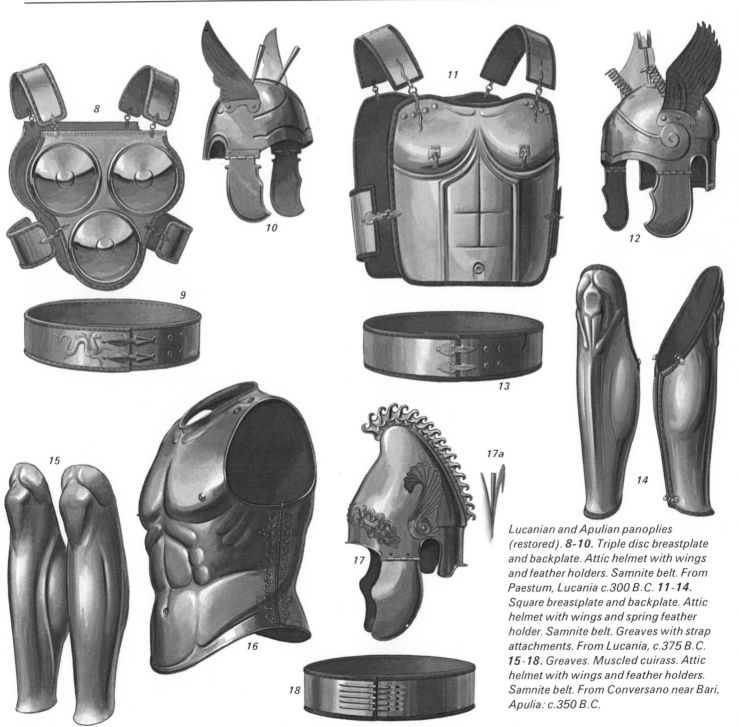

Lucanian and Apulian panoplies (restored). 8-10. Triple disc breastplate and backplate. Attic helmet with wings and feather holders. Samnite belt. From Paestum, Lucania c.300 B.C. 11-14. Square breastplate and backplate. Attic helmet with wings and spring feather holder. Samnite belt. Greaves with strap attachments. From Lucania, c.375 B.C. 15-18. Greaves. Muscled cuirass. Attic helmet with wings and feather holders. Samnite belt. From Conversano near Bari, Apulia: c.350 B.C.

The Later Etruscans

The Etruscans enter the war

At this point events took an unexpected turn. The Greek cities of southern Italy and Sicily had often called in Greek generals to help against their enemies. The cry for help had gone out from the Syracusans, and Acrotatus of Sparta had answered. On his way to Sicily he had briefly interfered in affairs in Illyria. He had now arrived at Taranto on his way to Sicily. For a moment the Samnites feared that he might use his forces against them and slowed down their drive north.

Their hesitation was just enough to swing the

▲ *1. Warrior in lamellar armour from Tarquinii. 2. The lamellar cuirass on the Mars, from Todi. 3. Warriors in flexible and muscled cuirasses from Chiusi. 4. Warrior in a quilted cuirass with scales: from Volterra. 4a. Detail of quilting. 5. Warrior in linen cuirass from Tarquinii.*

The conquest of southern Etruria

During the 4th century B.C. and the beginning of the 3rd, the Romans made a slow but relentless incursion into Etruria. Rome had lost her foot-hold in southern Etruria as a result of the Gallic invasion. Now she set about a reconquest. It took three years. This reconquest brought her into collision with Tarquinii and the other central Etruscan cities who were becoming fearful of Rome's growing power. In 388 B.C. and again in 386 Tarquinii took up arms but failed to drive the Romans back.

In 359 B.C. Tarquinii launched an invasion of Roman Etruria. Two years later Falerii joined in and the following year the rest of the Etruscan federation also took up arms. A pitiless war followed in which both sides massacred prisoners. Finally in 351 Rome brought Tarquinii and Falerii to their knees.

The end of the Etruscans

After the middle of the 4th century Rome no longer looked upon Etruria as a threat: the Etruscans were in a state of decline. In 311 they attacked the Roman fortress at Sutrium, in southern Etruria. The Romans easily won. Cortona, Perugia and Arezzo had to sign treaties.

At the beginning of the 3rd century the Etruscans made a last effort to throw off the Roman yoke, and joined forces with the Samnites, Umbrians and Celts. When the Samnites fell the Etruscans collapsed with them. During the first half of the 3rd century the rest of the Etruscan cities were either crushed or forced into alliance with Rome. Vulci fell in 280 B.C. and Volsinii in 265 B.C. Roman colonies were established in the heartland of Etruria and its days of greatness were over. When Hannibal arrived in 217 B.C. the Etruscans had no will to fight.

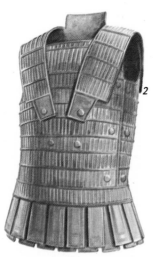

balance. The Romans counter-attacked. They threw all their available forces against the invading Samnite forces, and routed them.

The Samnites had come so near to winning. The war was to last another ten years but it had lost its momentum. In 311 B.C. several of the Etruscan cities entered the war but they were easily knocked out by the Romans. How different things might have been if they had entered the war three years earlier. In 304 B.C. the Samnites sued for peace and were left hardly worse off than before.

The peace only lasted six years. In 296 B.C., after two years of the usual skirmishings, the Samnites again made a lightning movement northwards. This time a Samnite army advanced through central Italy and joined forces with Etruscans, Umbrians and Gauls for an all-out assault on Rome. This caused near panic at Rome. At Sentinum the Samnite and Gallic armies faced the Roman legions. The battle was long drawn out, and the Romans only just won. The failure of the Etruscans and Umbrians to turn up for the battle probably cost them all their independence. Never again did Rome have serious competition from native Italians.

6. Sculpture of greaves and Montefortino helmet from Caere. 7. Etruscan Montefortino helmet. 8. Crude form of Attic helmet. 9. Restored greaves, muscled cuirass, Montefortino helmet, hoplite shield: from Orvieto. 10. Wall painting from a tomb at Tarquinii showing sword, shield, helmet and three heavy javelins (pila). 11. Head of a heavy pilum found in the walls at Grosseto.

Later Etruscan armour

During this period Etruria followed the Greek lead in armour and adopted the late classical styles. The stiff linen cuirasses were now often plated with bronze. This use of rectangular overlapping plates (lamellar) originated in Assyria. It is shown on wall paintings (far left, **1**) and on the famous statue of Mars from Todi (**2**). Experiments were made in flexible cuirasses of quilted linen reinforced with scale plates (**4**).

From the first half of the 4th century a new influence was felt: that of the Celts. The Senones, who arrived in Italy about 400 B.C., probably brought with them the Montefortino type of helmet (left, **7**). This was adopted by the Etruscans and Romans and became the commonest form of helmet from the 4th-1st century B.C. They appear on the 4th-century tomb of the reliefs at Cerveteri (**6**). A panoply from a 4th-century tomb near Lake Bolsena consists of a Greek style muscled cuirass, greaves and shield plus a Montefortino helmet (**9**). A very crude type of Attic helmet (**8**) became very common then all over Italy.

Weapons

The Greek hoplite sword continued in use. The most interesting development is the introduction of the heavy javelin (*pilum*). This is shown in a 4th-century Etruscan tomb at Tarquinii (**9**). The *pilum* had now become more important than the spear. This agrees with the tradition that the *pilum* was brought into general use against the Celts in the first half of the 4th century. The head of a heavy *pilum* (**11**) from Grosseto in Etruria probably comes from this period. The heavy *pilum* was set into a wooden shaft which was thickened at the junction and riveted into place. This formidable javelin became the main offensive weapon of the later Roman army.

Fortified Towns

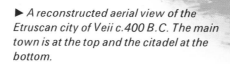

► *A reconstructed aerial view of the Etruscan city of Veii c.400 B.C. The main town is at the top and the citadel at the bottom.*

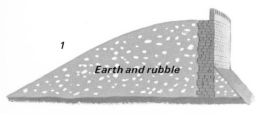

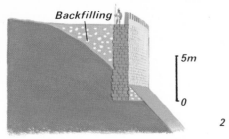

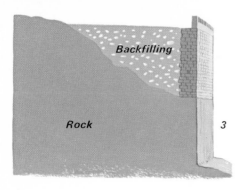

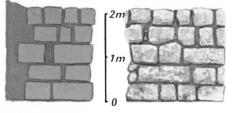

1, 2 and 3. Reconstructed sections of the Etruscan terrace walls at Veii.
1. The type used on level ground. The wall is set into a rampart of earth.
2. The type used on sloping ground.
3. The type used on cliffs. The cliff face is cut away and the wall built on top. The space behind the wall is filled with rubble and earth.
4. Section and face of the Veii walls.

Early fortifications

Most villages of 8th century B.C. Italy were on hill tops, just as in the rest of Europe. They usually relied on steep slopes for defence: where this was not enough, palisades and ditches were used.

There were hundreds of these hill-top villages in Etruria. With the rise of the Etruscan ruling class in the 7th century, groups of villages were united into formidable towns. Ramparts and ditches were gradually replaced by terrace walls.

The terrace walls of Veii

Excavations at the Etruscan town of Veii, 12km north of Rome, have revealed several stretches of the Etruscan walls. This unique form of wall is common to many Etruscan towns. Veii was built on a plateau defended by steep slopes at all but a few points (see large picture above).

Walls varying from 1.58m-2.08m thick have been uncovered at many points along the rim of the plateau. They date to the end of the 5th century B.C. just before the final Roman siege. These walls are made of rectangular blocks of stone about 45cm × 45cm in section and up to 1.38m long. Where the approach was flat walls just under 8m high, excluding battlements, were constructed with a steep ramp at the front to make it difficult for rams to be brought up. A massive mound at the back made it unbreachable (**1**, left).

Where there was a steep slope the wall was constructed a little distance down the hillside and then backfilled to level it off with the top of the plateau (**2**).

On a cliff face the rock was cut back to make it sheer. The wall was built on top, and backfilled as before (**3**). Some Etruscan walls had a ditch in front, sometimes cut out of the rock. At Luni a mound was erected crowned with a tower, where natural defences were weak.

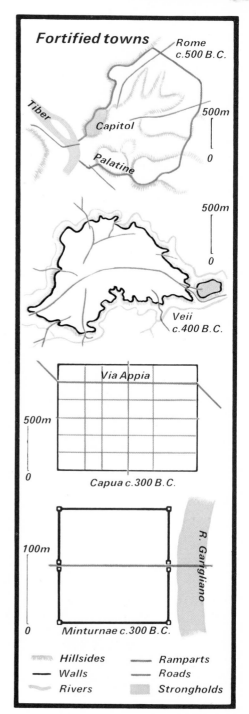

Fortified towns

Rome c.500 B.C.

Tiber

Capitol

Palatine

500m

Veii c.400 B.C.

500m

Via Appia

500m

Capua c.300 B.C.

100m

R. Garigliano

Minturnae c.300 B.C.

Hillsides	Ramparts
Walls	Roads
Rivers	Strongholds

Citadel

The early defences of Rome

Like the Etruscan cities Rome also grew out of a group of hill-top villages. The original site of Rome was the Palatine hill which rose out of the marshes on the left bank of the Tiber. Other hills in the area were also occupied. These were gradually united to form the city.

According to Dionysius, the Palatine, Aventine and Capitoline hills were fortified with palisades and ditches in the time of Romulus, c.750 B.C.

It was possibly the Etruscans who first gave the town one continuous line of defences. From this time the Capitoline Hill became the citadel. It was the only part of the city that did not fall to the Celts in 390 B.C. The Etruscans probably erected the massive eastern rampart (*agger*) with a ditch (*fossa*) in front, which stretched across the eastern side of the old city.

The walls of Servius Tullius

The ramparts of Rome may have been replaced by stone walls but these proved no protection against the Celts and in 378 B.C. Rome began to build the famous "Servian Wall". This wall was constructed of rectangular blocks of tufa 60cm high by 45cm-65cm thick and between 74cm and 210cm long. Across the weakly defended eastern side of the city they built a massive terrace wall 3.6m wide at the base, backed by an enormous rampart 10m high levelled off to form an artifical ridge. In front was a ditch 10m deep and 30m wide.

Types of walls and gates

Rectangular stone blocks were normally used in Etruria and Latium (see bottom far left). The hill peoples used more primitive polygonal masonry, (below right).

In Etruria and Latium the arched gate became almost universal. Where polygonal masonry was used, gateways often had sloping sides and were either pointed at the top or had a heavy lintel across.

Etruscan and Roman colonies

The Etruscans established many colonies in the lands they conquered. These were military and trading outposts. The prime objective of Roman colonies was military —to keep a foothold in enemy territory. The most famous of the Etruscan colonies was Capua in Campania. Like other Etruscan and Roman colonies, Capua was built on a rectangular grid. It was very large, covering two square kilometres. It is unlikely that the original settlement was this large, although extra space would have been allowed for trading activities. It is 80 times the size of typical Roman colonies like Minturnae.

▲ *Walls of polygonal masonry, Segni.*

◄ *Etrusco-Roman arched gate, S. Maria di Falleri.*

The Latin/Roman Army c.340 B.C.

Pyrrhus invades Italy

Rome now tried to force the Greek states of southern Italy to join her. Taranto, which was one of those being coerced, appealed to Pyrrhus, King of Epirus. In 280 B.C. Pyrrhus landed in southern Italy with 25,000 crack troops and 20 elephants. His aim was to unite Rome's enemies in the south. Before this could happen the Romans advanced with an army of about 25,000 men. At Heraclea the Romans faced a Macedonian phalanx for the first time and were defeated. But although they lost 7,000 men they inflicted such severe casualties on Pyrrhus, who

The Roman legions (c.340 B.C.)

During his account of the Latin war (340-338 B.C.) Livy gives us another glimpse of the legion. All legionaries used the oval shield *(scutum)*. The Greek style phalanx had been abandoned. The legion was split up into three lines.

The rear line had 15 companies *(ordines)*, each sub-divided into three parts. At the front were the best of the veterans *(triarii)*. Behind these came the *rorarii* and at the rear the reserves *(accensi)*. All were spearmen. Each of these three parts consisted of 60 men, two centurions and a standard bearer.

The middle line *(principes)* was made up of 15 units or maniples. These were the cream of the army. The front line *(hastati)* were also divided into 15 maniples. The *principes* and *hastati* were armed with swords and heavy javelins. Attached to each maniple of *hastati* were 20 skirmishers *(leves)* armed with a spear and javelin. The legion strength was 5,000. Each unit of the back line had 186 men. Each unit of the *principes* and *hastati* had about 64 men.

The forty-five unit legion

Most scholars have rejected Livy's description or revised it to conform to the pattern of the later legion. However, the Roman army was constantly in a state of development. Livy's legion is half-way between the Etruscan army and that described by Polybius (c.150 B.C.)

The origins of this 45 unit legion may be seen in the army of Servius Tullius (p.15). Before Servius Tullius, the 90 centuries of classes 2-5 were Latin. When Rome joined the Latin League she reverted to the 2x45 units of this original Latin army.

The class system remained in some of the names: *principes* were the first class (although they now fought in the second line) and *triarii* were the third class.

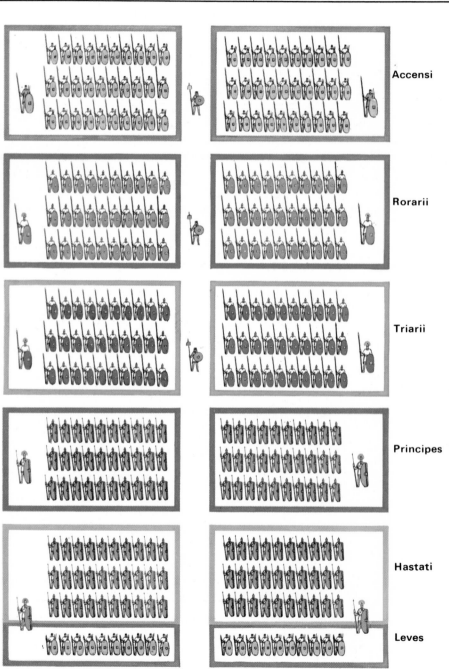

Accensi

Rorarii

Triarii

Principes

Hastati

Leves

▲ The units of the Roman-Latin army, as described by Livy. The double centuries of accensi, rorarii and triarii *formed one* ordo. *The* principes *and* hastati *each formed a maniple. It is uncertain how many centurions there were to a maniple.*

could not replace his losses, that "a Pyrrhic victory" became proverbial for winning at excessive cost.

The following year Rome dispatched 40,000 troops against Pyrrhus. This time Pyrrhus was supported by the southern Italians. The second battle lasted two days and its result was much the same.

Depressed at his losses, Pyrrhus crossed over to Sicily to help the Greeks against the Carthaginians. Anticipating this, the Carthaginians had arranged an alliance with Rome. Pyrrhus almost drove the Carthaginians out of Sicily, confining them to the port of Lilybaeum (now Marsala) at the western tip.

At the prospect of a long siege, Pyrrhus once more lost interest and decided to return to Italy.

For more than two years Pyrrhus had been in Sicily. The Romans had not wasted this precious breathing space. They had forced the Samnites and Lucanians into submission, so that when Pyrrhus returned he was on his own. The two Roman consuls were separated and Pyrrhus tried to engage them one at a time. He attacked one army but failed to gain a victory and retreated to Taranto. Soon afterwards he sailed back to Epirus. He had never been defeated, but he had lost the war and with it two-thirds of his army.

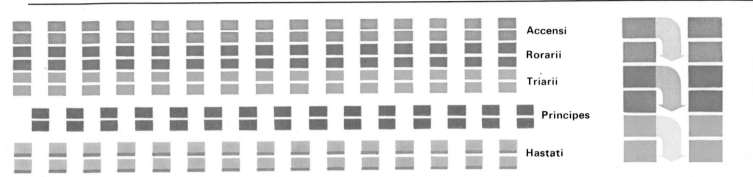

Accensi

Rorarii

Triarii

Principes

Hastati

Battle formation

In the new army the prime offensive weapon of the legionary was the heavy javelin *(pilum)*. The old spearmen still exist in the *triarii*, *rorarii* and *accensi*. But over a third of the army had been moved out front, armed with *pila* to break up the enemy.

The three lines are drawn up like the black squares on a chess board. The 15 centuries of *hastati* are at the front with a gap between each. The *principes* are drawn up similarly covering the gaps. The units of the back line in the same way cover the gaps in the *principes*' line.

In battle

The battle starts with the skirmishers *(leves)* trying to break up the enemy formation with their light javelins. As the enemy advances, the light-armed withdraw through the gaps and the *hastati* charge, throwing their heavy javelins and then closing in with their swords. If this fails to break the enemy, they retreat into the gaps between the *principes*, who similarly charge. If both lines are beaten they withdraw on the *triarii* and retire through the gaps in the line. The *triarii* then close the gaps, and the whole army retreats. The method by which the gaps might be closed is shown on the right above. This manoeuvre is discussed in greater detail on p.68 ("The manipular tactic".)

The veterans *(triarii)*

Whilst the *hastati* and *principes* were fighting, the veterans *(triarii)* knelt on one knee with their left leg forward. Their large oval shields rested against their left shoulders covering them from enemy missiles. Their spear butts were stuck in the ground with the spear pointing obliquely forward, "like a palisade", Livy says. Only if all else had failed did they enter the battle.

It is noteworthy that the standards were with the rear line so that if the units operating out front were scattered they knew which *ordines* to fall back on. Livy does not tell us whether there were one or two centurions to each maniple of *principes* and *hastati*, or none.

The defensive character of the legion

During the first 200 years of the republic Rome probably suffered many defeats. The patriotic Livy usually says that "bad weather stopped play" to account for the Romans not gaining a victory. The greatest of these defeats was the disaster at the Allia (390 B.C.). These defeats, and the Allia in particular, may account for the strongly defensive character of the 4th-century legion. The more mobile formation was probably an answer to the fast-moving armies of the Celts and Samnites. The javelin throwers at the front may have been particularly designed to break the Celtic charge.

▲ *A legion (left) drawn up ready for battle with gaps between each of the units to allow the lines to interchange. Right: how the* ordines *might fill the gaps by moving up the rear centuries.*

▲ *The* triarii *kneeling under cover of their shields whilst the* hastati *and* principes *are fighting.*

The Carthaginians

Rome now controlled the whole of peninsular Italy. The legions had faced up to the Macedonian phalanx under the command of one of the greatest generals of all time. The legionaries had shown that they were equal to anything the world could produce. In the north they had come face to face with the dreaded Celts and defeated them decisively. It was only a matter of time before Rome settled accounts there for good. In the south she now gazed across the straits of Messina to Sicily. It was inevitable that Rome's expansion southwards would bring her into head-on collision with the great naval power of the western Mediterranean, Carthage, which had colonized western Sicily.

How Rome became involved in a war with Carthage is very confused. In 264 B.C. the Romans crossed the straits of Messina, and the longest and bitterest war she had yet fought had begun.

Over the next 120 years Rome waged three wars against the Carthaginians. These were the hardest-fought wars in Roman history. In fact Carthage was the only real opponent that Rome ever came up against. During these wars Rome lost half a million men. At the end she completely defeated the Carthaginians, and ploughed the city of Carthage into the ground. In the last few years the first full-scale excavations have started on the site of ancient Carthage and at last a true picture of the great city is coming to light.

For this period we are fortunate to have the writings of the great Greek historian, Polybius. He was a soldier and fully understood the military systems of his time.

◀ *Hannibal's army crossing the Alps. Hannibal, at the head of his bodyguard, tries to force his way through the attacking Celts. The scene is set in the Durance defile just south of Briançon.*

Carthage and her Harbours

The Romans invade Africa

Rome realized that if she were to stand a chance of beating Carthage she must build a navy. Since the Carthaginian ships were considered the best, an abandoned Carthaginian ship was used as a prototype. Within two months a fleet of 120 was launched. The Romans developed a boarding plank with which they locked ships together so that they could be easily boarded, thus turning a naval battle into an infantry battle. This was so successful that they soon gained control of the sea.

As Carthage was compelled to fight the superb

▲ *Aerial view of the Carthaginian promontory showing the harbours; **H, H,** and the wall across the isthmus; **W, W.** An approximation to the ancient coastline is marked in red.*

The Phoenician capital in the west

Carthage was built on a small promontory jutting out into the sea just north of Tunis. The city began its life as a haven for Phoenician trading ships about the same time as the founding of Rome. Carthage grew rapidly. By the end of the 7th century B.C. she had established herself as the leading Phoenician colony in the west.

Attempts to establish colonies in Sicily and Sardinia brought Carthage into conflict with the Greeks. In alliance with the Etruscans, she decisively defeated the Greeks in a naval battle off the coast of Corsica (c.535 B.C.) and managed to exclude the Greeks from the two northern islands. In Sicily, however, Greek and Carthaginian were at each other's throats for 300 years.

Carthage also gained a foothold in Spain. Her influence there was weakened during the first war with Rome, but between the first and second wars, through the efforts of the Barca family, she gained control of most of south east Spain, and founded a capital at Cartagena.

The walls of Carthage

The site of Carthage is shaped like an arrowhead joined to the coast by an isthmus about 4.5km wide.

At the end of the third war with Rome (146 B.C.). Carthage was destroyed. The Romans made such a thorough job that until recently no trace of the ancient walls had been found. Furthermore, a long stretch of the ancient sea wall has sunk beneath the water. This can be seen from the air. In 1949 the French army discovered part of the Carthaginian defences across the isthmus. There was a ditch about 20m deep backed by a rampart surmounted with a palisade. Upright timbers supporting the bank and palisade were sunk into the bedrock.

The Greek historian Appian, in his account of the third war, tells us that Carthage had triple walls about 15m high and 10m wide, with four-storey towers every 60m. Stables for 300 elephants and 4,000 horses were built into the walls. There were barracks for 24,000 soldiers. Only the archaeologist's spade can tell us how much truth there is in this. In 1974 an international rescue dig began at Carthage, in an attempt to discover something of the ancient city before it is completely built over. When these excavations are complete we may have a picture of what ancient Carthage was really like.

▼ *Aerial view of the harbour area of Carthage showing the horseshoe and lozenge-shaped ponds. Where the sea wall has sunk can be seen in dark blue.*

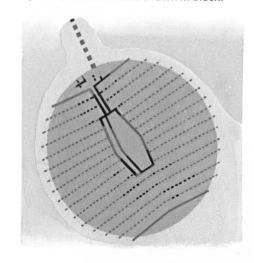

▼ *A reconstructed plan of Dr Hurst's excavations on the island of the military harbour. The structure in the middle is the admiral's house. The dotted lines are ship-sheds. Remains are shown in black.*

Roman infantry on land and at sea, she went over to the defensive. The war declined into a series of long drawn-out sieges of Carthaginian strongholds.

In 256 B.C. the Romans launched an invasion of Africa. The consul Regulus with 15,000 foot and 500 cavalry landed about four days' march from Carthage. Twice in the following months Regulus defeated the ill-trained Carthaginian forces. He set up his winter quarters at Tunis, within sight of the great city. During the winter the Carthaginians sued for peace but Regulus set such harsh terms that they were left no alternative but to fight on.

The great harbours

The pride of Carthage was her great harbours, one commercial and one military. Appian describes them. The two ports were placed one behind the other, separated by a double wall. The front port was for merchant ships. It had an entrance to the sea about 20m wide which could be closed with iron chains. Behind this port was the military harbour, which had access to the sea through the commercial harbour.

Within the military harbour was an island. The island and the harbour were packed with ship-sheds and stores: enough for 200 ships. Two columns stood at the entrance to each dock. These gave the appearance of a continuous portico to the harbour and the island. On the island stood the admiral's house. This rose high above the level of the surrounding buildings and enabled the naval commander to see what was going on out at sea.

The excavation of the military harbour

There are two ponds, one horseshoe and one lozenge shaped. These have long been thought to be the harbours. In 1974 the British archaeologist, Dr Henry Hurst, began excavating the horseshoe pond, with remarkable results. In the centre he uncovered the foundations of a large building, and radiating from this, rows of rectangular stone blocks. These rows which are 5.9m apart can only be the foundations of ship-sheds.

Over 100 years ago Beulé, the French archaeologist, found similar rows of blocks on the north side of the pond.

The edge of the later Roman harbour has also been found. If it coincided with the earlier quayside then the harbour would have had a circuit of over 1,100m: sufficient for about 160 ship-sheds. There are 30 on the island. There can be little doubt that Appian's description was fundamentally right.

▲ A cut-away section of a reconstructed ship-shed. (As no tiles have been found, the roof is shown flat).

▼ A reconstruction of the military harbour showing the ship-sheds and the admiral's house. Only the island has so far been excavated. The reconstruction is based on the drawings of Dr H. R. Hurst and S. C. Gibson.

The Carthaginian Navy

Defeat, disaster and humiliation for Rome
In their desperation the Carthaginians called in a Spartan officer. During the winter he drilled the Carthaginian army and knocked them into shape.

In the spring he marched out his troops and offered battle to the Romans. He lined up his phalanx with 100 elephants in front and 4,000 cavalry on the wings. The Romans were shattered by the elephants, which were followed up by the phalanx. On the wings the African cavalry drove the Roman horsemen from the field and attacked the legions from the rear. Only 2,000 Romans escaped. The consul Regulus and 500

Carthaginian ships

It was Carthage's fleet which gave her control of the western Mediterranean. Unfortunately very little is known about it. We know from Polybius that the prime fighting ship was the quinquereme (a galley with five banks of oars) because the Romans copied them. We know that one of her fleets had a seven banker as flag ship. (This ship was captured from Pyrrhus.) We also know they had triremes (three banks of oars) and quadriremes (four banks).

The size of the fleet

Appian tells us that the naval harbour at Carthage had docks for 200 ships. As we have seen, he was probably right. But this could only have been part of the Carthaginian navy. There must have been smaller fleets permanently stationed at such places as Palermo and Lilybaeum in Sicily. Polybius says that in 256 B.C. Carthage put to sea a fleet of 350 decked warships. In battle these ships would have been drawn up several rows deep.

▼ *Section of the quinquereme on the right. It shows the position of the three oars and five oarsmen. Scale 1:150.*

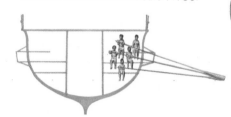

Mass produced ships

In 1971 the hull of a Carthaginian galley was discovered in shallow water just north of the port of Lilybaeum. This ship, and another which was discovered nearby, have been dated to the period of the first war with Rome. The shipwright's marks on the timbers imply that they were mass produced, which would explain how Rome could build 120 ships in two months.

▼ *1. Part of the hull of the first of two Carthaginian warships discovered near Lilybaeum in Sicily. 2. Part of the ram of the second ship. A. Method of joining planks together with tenons and dowels. B. Method of nailing planks to ribs. C and D. Sections of keel. E. Section of rearmost rib. F. Section of fifth rib showing planking nailed to rib and keel. G and H. Sections of ram.*

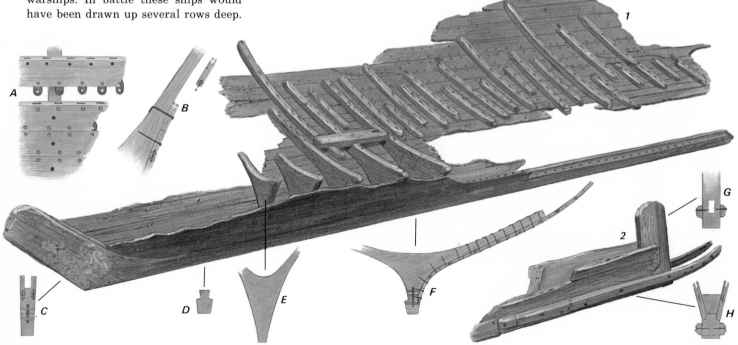

men were captured. But worse was to come. The Roman fleet, now 330 strong, was ordered to pick up the survivors. On the way back it was caught in a storm, and all but 80 ships were destroyed with a loss of perhaps 100,000 lives.

Far from giving up, the Romans built another fleet. They now laid siege to the port of Lilybaeum at the western end of Sicily. The legions surrounded the port on land and the navy operated a blockade at sea. To the humiliation of the Roman navy, a Carthaginian captain called Hannibal the Rhodian continually slipped through the blockade in a fast galley. The heavy Roman ships could not capture him, and soon others were following his example. By building sandbanks in the harbour entrance the Romans managed to capture one of the blockade runners and finally overhauled the Rhodian in it.

By 248 B.C. both sides were exhausted. That year the Romans did no more than hold their lines. The Carthaginians were just as inactive. The next year a young Carthaginian general, Hamilcar Barca, was put in command. By raiding the Italian coast he hoped to draw the Romans away from Lilybaeum: he failed. The war in Sicily came to a standstill.

◀ *Section of quinquereme showing rowing positions. Below: front of a Carthaginian war galley, on a coin.*

▼ *Reconstruction of a quinquereme without lead sheathing on the hull, or bronze on ram. Right: the front of fully-clad ship.*

The Lilybaeum wrecks
Parts of the Lilybaeum wrecks are shown left: (1) is the stern of the first ship. The other, (2) is part of the ram of the second. The keel is made of maple, the ribs of oak and the planking and tusk-like pieces on the ram are of pine.

The ships are carvel built: the outside planking was assembled first, and the ribs inserted afterwards. The planks were joined with flat tongues of wood (tenons) which were held in place with dowels (**A**). The planking was nailed to the ribs from the outside and the nail bent over on the inside (**B**). The caulking (stopping up the seams) was done with a putty-like substance. The hull was then covered with lead sheeting. The ram was encased in bronze.

What type of ship?
The excavator, Honor Frost, believes that both these ships were *liburna* (singular, *liburnum*) which were fast, light ships. This may be so but it must be pointed out that the estimated size of one ship, about 35m long and 5m wide, is quite large. The ship-sheds at Carthage which were only 5·9m wide must have held quinqueremes.

The reconstruction of a quinquereme
The main interest of the Lilybaeum ships is their structure. This has been used for the reconstruction of a quinquereme (above). The superstructure is based on a Carthaginian coin from Spain (left) and a carving from Carthage (right). Both show what is unmistakably an outrigger behind the eye. This structure projects from each side to give the oars greater leverage. Both also show the deck above this. The coin shows oval shields strapped along the railing. The Lilybaeum type of ram is shown on Trajan's column (right).

The quinquereme probably had oars at 3 levels, with two men to each of the upper oars and one man to the lower oar (see *The Roman Army*, p.22).

Polybius says that the Carthaginian fleet of 350 decked ships must have had 150,000 crew. By this he implies that the Carthaginian ships, like the Roman, carried 300 seamen and 120 marines. About 270 of the seamen were rowers.

Carving from Carthage showing the front of a war galley. The ram shown on this and on the coin on the left is the most common form. The Lilybaeum type is shown on the sculpture of a Roman galley from Trajan's column below.

Hannibal's Army: The Africans

The Carthaginians had grown weary of the war and became lax in sending supply fleets to their beleagured garrisons. In the spring of 241 B.C. the Roman fleet intercepted and destroyed the belated supply fleet. The starving garrisons were at the mercy of the Romans, and surrendered. They were forced to leave Sicily entirely and pay a war indemnity.

After the war, the Carthaginian mercenaries who had been in Sicily mutinied. Carthage completely mismanaged the situation and but for Hamilcar

▲ 1-4. Hellenistic sculpture and painting. 1 and 3. Helmets from Pergamon, Turkey. 2. Officer from Magnesia-ad-Maeandrum, Turkey. 4. Helmet from a Macedonian grave. 5. A Carthaginian pikeman from Hannibal's army. He has typical Hellenistic equipment: Thracian helmet, strap-on greaves, round shield about 60cm in diameter and heavy spear 5m to 7m long. His shield is attached at his arm and controlled by a neck strap. His cuirass is Italian, part of the spoils captured from the Romans at Trebbia or Trasimeno.

The Carthaginian army

Most troops serving in the Carthaginian army were foreign mercenaries. There was, however, a nucleus of both infantry and cavalry who were half-castes (Liby-Phoenicians). This information is given by Polybius. He does not say how many. The answer may be in the barracks built into the walls of Carthage, for 20,000 infantry and 4,000 cavalry.

These half-castes formed a Macedonian type phalanx. The phalangite would have had the armour and weapons of a typical Hellenistic (late Greek) infantryman: a small round shield, a heavy two-handed spear 5m to 7m long and a short sword for hand-to-hand fighting. These pikemen would line up many ranks deep with several rows of spears projecting beyond the front rank.

On the sculpted Carthaginian galley shown on p.39 there is a standard crowned with a disc and crescent. This symbol's frequent appearance suggests it was the standard of Carthage.

The mercenaries

Mercenaries formed the bulk of any Carthaginian army. They came from many sources. There were Celts, Spaniards, Balearic Islanders (who were famous for their slingers), Ligurians, half-caste Greeks—mainly deserters and runaway slaves—and North Africans. Carthaginian discipline must have been imposed on these troops who probably served under Carthaginian officers.

The remarkable success of Hannibal whose army was 40 per cent Celtic is a tribute to the Carthaginian system. No attempt was made at uniformity. Each native group fought in its own way and had to be used to its best advantage. Hannibal's relationship with his troops was remarkable. In spite of their mixed backgrounds they stuck with him for fifteen years with never the whisper of a mutiny.

Massacred mercenaries

There is an unlikely story told by Diodorus that in 203 B.C. Hannibal killed the mercenaries who would not go to Africa with him. Hannibal could never have shipped more than a few of his men to Africa. He had no navy. The Romans probably offered terms to the bulk of Hannibal's army which had been left behind, then slaughtered them.

Barca would have been totally defeated. Hamilcar put down the revolt with utter ruthlessness, and completely routed the mutineers.

In the confusion Rome annexed Sardinia, with complete disregard for the treaty she had just signed.

Hamilcar Barca, disgusted with the policies of his government, which had betrayed the army in Sicily, left his native land and, taking his young son Hannibal with him, set out for Spain. Hamilcar met his death in action eight years later. By that time he had already conquered south-eastern Spain.

The Greek city of Marseilles, which had trading interests in Spain, was a Roman ally. On her behalf Rome forced Hasdrubal, Hamilcar's successor, to sign a treaty agreeing not to advance beyond the river Ebro. In 221 B.C., Hamilcar's son Hannibal, now 25 years old, was elected general by the troops.

Two years later Hannibal launched an attack on the lofty hill fort of Saguntum which the Romans had placed under their protection. He knew that the Romans would use this as a pretext for war, which they declared the following spring. The Romans began mobilising two armies, one for Spain, and one to invade Africa.

▶ *Numidian cavalryman shown on Trajan's Column, Rome.*

▼ *A Numidian horseman. The horse has no bridle or saddle. The man has javelins and round shield but no armour.*

The Numidians

The part of north Africa which we call Algeria was known to the Romans as Numidia, after the nomadic tribes who lived there. The camel had not yet been introduced into north Africa. In fact these tribesmen lived on horseback. They used no bridle or bit and rode bare-back. They made wonderful light cavalry: in fact they were so good that whoever controlled them would win a north African war. Scipio Africanus' greatest achievement was to persuade the Numidians to change sides at the end of the war with Hannibal. The change was decisive, and Hannibal lost.

When at the end of the second century B.C. Rome became involved in a war with the Numidians, they were so hard to conquer that the career of more than one Roman general came to an end because of his inability to win a decisive victory.

Numidian tactics and equipment

Numidian cavalry were useless as shock troops but were superb in a skirmish or in the pursuit of a fleeing enemy. At the battle of Cannae they could not break Rome's allied cavalry, but the moment this had been achieved by the Celts and Spaniards the pursuit was left to the Numidians. They would dart in towards the enemy, throw their javelins and retreat, making sure never to come into close contact. Again and again the Carthaginians used the Numidians to draw enemies into an ambush.

The Numidians appear on Trajan's Column in Rome, pursuing Dacians. Their horses have nothing but a neck strap. The riders have a round shield and short tunic, but wear no armour. Samples of iron javelin heads and pointed iron butts have been found in a 2nd-century B.C. prince's grave in Algeria.

Hannibal's Army: The Spaniards

Hannibal marches on Italy

Hannibal had other plans. His aim was to lead a revolt against Rome in Italy. As the Romans controlled the sea, he must reach Italy by land.

First he had to delay Scipio, who was in charge of the invasion of Spain. He managed to engineer a revolt in northern Italy, and Scipio's legions were detached to deal with it.

Leaving strong forces to defend Spain and north Africa, Hannibal fought his way north to the Pyrenees. Before Scipio could collect together a fresh army, he had control of north-eastern Spain.

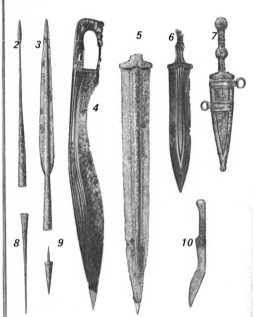

▲ *1.* A saunion, *heavy javelin with barbed point made entirely of iron. 2.* Pilum *type Javelin head. 3. Spear head. 4. Falcata. 5. Straight cut and thrust sword (Gladius Hispaniensis). 6. Dagger. 7. Dagger with scabbard. 8 and 9. Spear butts. 10. Knife of the type that was fixed to the* falcata *scabbard. These are all 4th-2nd century B.C. Spanish weapons. Scale 1:8.*

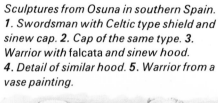

Sculptures from Osuna in southern Spain. 1. Swordsman with Celtic type shield and sinew cap. 2. Cap of the same type. 3. Warrior with falcata *and sinew hood. 4. Detail of similar hood. 5. Warrior from a vase painting.*

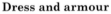

Spanish infantry

Spanish infantry and cavalry formed a small but important part of Hannibal's army. Of the 20,000 infantry who reached Italy, 8,000 were Spanish. Hannibal used two types of Spanish infantry: swordsmen and slingers. The latter came from the Balearic Islands off the coast of Spain. Polybius tells us that the swordsmen wore short white tunics bordered with purple—by this he probably means crimson. They had a large Celtic type of shield and a short cut-and-thrust sword. Sculptures from Osuna in south Spain show warriors who fit Polybius' description well (**1**, **3**, above).

Weapons

The Spanish sword gained immortality when the Romans adopted it. The legionary sword was known as *Gladius Hispaniensis*. This was the pointed sword (**5** above). The commonest type found in Spain was the elegant curved *falcata* (**4**). This was a cut-and-thrust weapon. The average length of a *falcata* blade was only 45cm. It is clear from a fragment of a statue (not shown here) that the sword hung on the left side. These swords sometimes had a short knife attached to the scabbard.

A large number of daggers have also been found (**6**, **7**). These are the forerunners of the Roman dagger. The Spanish also used a short *pilum*. The most extraordinary weapon was the *saunion* (**1**). This was a barbed javelin made entirely of iron.

Dress and armour

The two warriors from Osuna have spined Celtic type shields. This was the type described by Polybius. There was also a small round shield which is often shown on sculptures. A short tunic and broad belt is shown on hundreds of figurines. Belt clasps are also common.

Figure 3, above, is wearing a striking crested head gear, shown more clearly on another sculpture (**4**). The Greek geographer Strabo tells us that the Iberians wore caps of sinew. This is probably what is shown here. The crest proves that it cannot be hair. These hoods are very similar to those shown on sculptures found in south-west France. The caps shown on (**1**) and (**2**) seem to be a simplified version of these hoods. A few bronze helmets have been found but they are very rare.

Scipio finally sailed for Marseilles, Rome's ally. On his arrival there he was astonished to learn that Hannibal was no longer in Spain but was advancing towards the river Rhône. He could only assume that Hannibal was heading for Marseilles to knock out Rome's halfway house.

Four days after leaving the coast, Hannibal arrived at the Rhône. He had with him 38,000 infantry, 8,000 cavalry and 34 elephants. Scipio received the news and sent his cavalry north to report on Hannibal's movements. On the opposite side of the river the Celts had assembled in force. Hannibal was able to outflank them by secretly sending part of his cavalry to cross the river further north, and managed to force his way across.

The outflanking movement had taken several precious days. Hannibal felt sure that Scipio must be approaching and he still had to get his elephants across. He dispatched some of his Numidians south to check on the Roman movements. The same day they returned to say that they had fallen in with the Roman cavalry. Hannibal felt sure this was the cavalry screen ahead of the legions. He dared not risk a battle before he reached Italy.

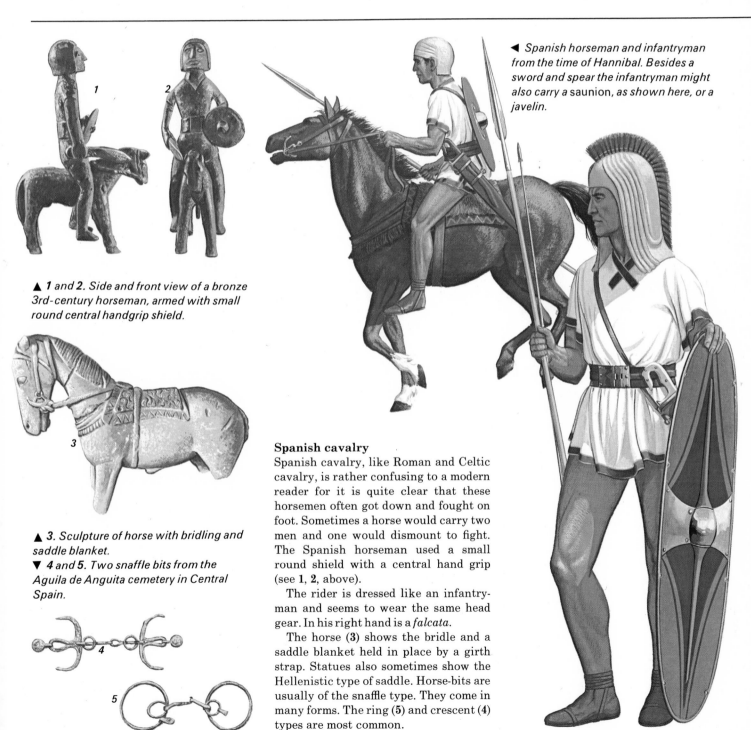

◀ *Spanish horseman and infantryman from the time of Hannibal. Besides a sword and spear the infantryman might also carry a* saunion, *as shown here, or a javelin.*

▲ *1 and 2. Side and front view of a bronze 3rd-century horseman, armed with small round central handgrip shield.*

▲ *3. Sculpture of horse with bridling and saddle blanket.*

▼ *4 and 5. Two snaffle bits from the Aguila de Anguita cemetery in Central Spain.*

Spanish cavalry

Spanish cavalry, like Roman and Celtic cavalry, is rather confusing to a modern reader for it is quite clear that these horsemen often got down and fought on foot. Sometimes a horse would carry two men and one would dismount to fight. The Spanish horseman used a small round shield with a central hand grip (see 1, 2, above).

The rider is dressed like an infantryman and seems to wear the same head gear. In his right hand is a *falcata*.

The horse (3) shows the bridle and a saddle blanket held in place by a girth strap. Statues also sometimes show the Hellenistic type of saddle. Horse-bits are usually of the snaffle type. They come in many forms. The ring (5) and crescent (4) types are most common.

Hannibal's Army: The Elephants

Hannibal races northwards

Hannibal had been heading for the shortest and easiest route to Italy—up the Durance valley and over the Montgenèvre Pass. Now, believing that the Romans were close, he decided to march up the Rhône in an attempt to lose them.

The next morning he placed his cavalry as a screen against the advancing legions and sent his infantry on up the river. During the day he managed to get the elephants across on rafts and soon caught up with his infantry.

The Roman cavalry advanced far enough north to

see Hannibal's camp and then returned in all haste to the coast to report.

Scipio could hardly credit the news they brought. It could mean only one thing. The Carthaginian army was not heading for Marseilles but Italy. In near panic, Scipio and his legions raced northwards. By the time they reached the deserted camp Hannibal had been gone three days. Realizing that Italy lay wide open, Scipio dashed back to the coast. There was no time to transport his army back so he ordered his brother to take the soldiers on to Spain whilst he sailed for Italy.

Hannibal had been marching northward for four days when he heard of Scipio's retreat. The army had now reached the point where the Rhône is joined by the Isère. The two rivers formed a great triangle of land known as "the Island". The army turned into the Alps, following the Isère until it was joined by the Drac. Then they turned south to cross the low pass that would bring them back to the Durance valley. Here the local tribes attacked them and the army suffered many casualties in forcing their way through. But within a few days they had rejoined the broad open valley of the Durance.

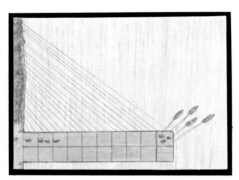

◄ *Hannibal's elephants being towed across the Rhône on rafts. According to Polybius, several fell into the water and waded across with their trunks above water. Several* mahouts *(elephant drivers) drowned but the elephants got across. The inset shows the jetty made of rafts 8m wide, moored to trees on the bank. When the elephants reached the last two rafts, they were cut free and towed across by boats.*

► *A Carthaginian coin showing an African war elephant. He is identifiable by his big ears and saddle back.*

Indians and Africans

War elephants were first brought to the west at the time of Alexander the Great, c.325 B.C. They had a devastating effect against cavalry until horses got used to them. These elephants were imported from India. States such as Egypt and Carthage which did not have direct contact with India found it very difficult to obtain supplies. However, there was an alternative—the north African forest elephant which is now extinct. This elephant was smaller than the other species, measuring less than 2·5m at the shoulder, whereas the Indian is about 3m and the great African bush elephant is 3·5m.

Carthaginian war elephants

The Carthaginians hunted the forest elephant in Morocco and Algeria, and on the edge of the Sahara desert 800km to the south. Elephants were introduced during the first war with Rome in 262 B.C. and were used against infantry as well as cavalry. They shattered Roman morale and for a long time the legionaries would not face them. They won their laurels in 255 B.C. when they trampled Regulus' infantry into the dust at the Bagradas plains.

Hannibal's elephants

Once the legionaries had captured some elephants and learned their weak spots they ceased to play an important role. Even so, Hannibal tried to bring 34 of them to Italy. All except one of these died either during the Alpine crossing or in the bitter winter that followed. At the Trebbia (218 B.C.), the only battle in which they fought, they played a minor part as they were set against the Roman cavalry which were massively outnumbered anyway.

Crossing the Rhône

The elephants were terrified of the fast-flowing Rhône which is between 200m and 500m wide, and flows at about five metres a second. The Carthaginians built several solid rafts about eight metres wide. They lashed two of these together and moored them to the bank. By adding others tied to the trees they managed to build a jetty 16m wide and 60m long. Two very strong rafts were tied to the end. They then covered it all with earth to look like the riverside path. With two females they managed to lure the other elephants on to the jetty. Once on the end rafts, they were cut loose and towed across the river.

Crossing the Alps

The valley of death

A few days' march up the Durance valley brought the army to L'Argentière-la-Bessée. Here the river passes a narrow gorge and the road takes to the hills. Hannibal advanced, with cavalry at the front, infantry in the rear and baggage in the middle.

When part of the army was stretched out along the hillside the Celts attacked the rear. The infantry faced about and fought a rearguard action. The Celts now appeared above them, pelting them with stones and rolling huge boulders down the hillside on to the army.

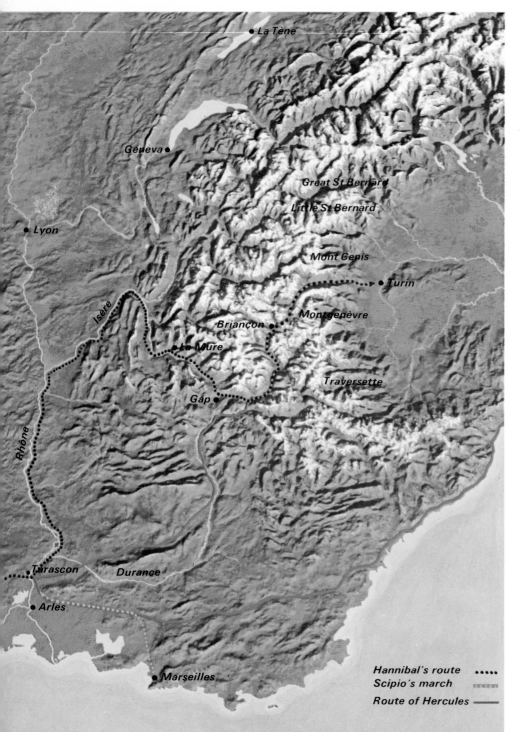

Hannibal's route ·····
Scipio's march ┅┅┅
Route of Hercules ———

The Rhône crossing

Hannibal intended to use the fabled route of Hercules to Italy: up the Durance valley and over the Montgenèvre pass into Italy. It was the easiest way, and the age-old trade route between northern Italy and Spain. Hannibal followed it until he reached the Rhône at Tarascon. This was the lowest point at which the Rhône could be crossed. The area to the south was flooded until recent times. When the Romans laid their road from Nîmes to Arles they had to build a viaduct across these marshes (known later as 'Le Pont des Arcs').

"The Island"

After crossing the river Hannibal abandoned his original route and marched northward hoping to lose Scipio's army. By the time he received news of Scipio's departure he had marched four days up the Rhône. Here he came to a place called "the Island," a triangle of land bordered on two sides by the Rhône and the River Skaras. It was blocked at its far end by an inpenetrable range of mountains and extensive marshes. This stretch of land is easy to recognise: it lies between the Rhône and the Isère. The Roman name for the Isère, Isara, is very similar to Skaras.

Livy and Polybius

Livy names some tribes encountered by Hannibal. Attempts to identify Hannibal's route by using the position of these tribes in the Roman Empire is fruitless. The Rhône valley was constantly in turmoil as wave after wave of barbarian invaders swept down, driving all others before them.

From "the Island" Hannibal turned into the Alps. It is difficult to make the accounts of Livy and Polybius agree. Livy's account is confused and it is safer to use Polybius as our guide.

Beyond the gorge the road descends to the valley. A huge rocky spur juts out leaving only a narrow passage. When the cavalry had passed this point the Celts launched an attack on the baggage train and cut the army in half. The infantry, and Hannibal with it, were trapped in the defile!

All night they struggled to get free. Not until the next morning did Hannibal manage to break out. His losses had been enormous. By that evening his sleepless infantry had struggled up to the pass. Here they camped for two days awaiting stragglers.

On the north side of the pass the snows of the previous year had not melted and the icy surface was now covered with fresh snow. As the soldiers descended, their feet sank through the snow and slid on the ice beneath, causing many to stumble and plunge into the ravine below. As if this was not enough, part of the road had been carried away by a landslide. The soldiers managed to build up the road sufficiently for the horses and baggage animals to get past but the elephants had to spend four nights on top of the freezing pass. Three days later the remnants of the Carthaginian army struggled into the valley of the Po.

Which pass?

Scholars have hotly disputed which pass Hannibal took. Polybius tells us that the passes of the Alps were snow-covered all the year. This is a general statement and must refer to passes in constant use: the Montgenèvre, the Little St Bernard and the Brenner. Scientists studying the changing climate agree that at that time the snow level in the Alps was much lower, about 2,000m. Today it is around 3,000m, so the pass was not necessarily a high one.

The pass that Hannibal used should accommodate the following points:
1. It should have a defile within a day's march (16-30km) of its summit.
2. The top of the pass should be large enough for an army to camp on.
3. The descent should be at least partially facing north. Snow and ice were encountered climbing down but not up.
4. It should have a precipitous descent.
5. The far side of the pass should be three days' march from the flat land.
6. One should see Italy from the top.

▲ The descent from the Montgenèvre pass. The landslide area where the road was broken is in the background.

The Montgenèvre Pass

Only one pass fits the last condition, the Traversette. However, apart from this it fits only condition four. Its defile is more than a day's march from the summit. It is also 2914m high, 900m above the estimated snow line of ancient times.

The Mont Cenis (2083m) and the Clapier (2482m) routes fit only conditions 1 and 2. It is impossible to see Italy from any point on the Clapier. The Little St Bernard (2188m) fits only conditions 2 and 4.

The only other reasonable contender is the Montgenèvre (1850m): it meets the first five conditions.

The Montgenèvre is therefore the obvious choice. It is also the lowest. This would certainly make sense as it was on Hannibal's original route. To get back on course from "the Island" he must have cut across the Alpine foothills.

The probable route

It is possible to reconstruct Hannibal's probable route from Polybius' account.

Polybius says Hannibal followed the river for 800 stades (160km), then began the ascent. By following the Isère then the Drac for 150km, one comes to a point near modern La Mure, where the route gets very difficult. Here the Celts tried to block his route. Beyond this the road is easy, going over gentle slopes by the Bayard (1248m) or Manse (1260m) passes back to the Durance valley. Six days' march from La Mure (about 150km) they would have reached the defile 10km south of Briançon. Here they were trapped. The following day they reached the summit of the pass 20km away. By this route, the distance from the Rhône crossing to the start of the ascent was 287km: Polybius says 1400 *stades* (280km). From there to the arrival in Italy (Avigliana) is 234km: Polybius says 1200 *stades* (240km).

▼ *The route to the Montgenèvre pass. The defile is at the bottom. The red dotted line is Hannibal's march. The blue arrows show the Celtic attack. The two large arrows are where the army was cut in half.*

Montgenèvre Pass

Briançon

The Celts

Seven years before Hannibal set out on his long march, the Celts of northern Italy had launched an all-out attack on Rome. The most violent of the Celtic tribes, the Senones, had long since disappeared. It was they who had sacked Rome in 390 B.C. Again and again over the next hundred years they had invaded central Italy. They had joined the Samnites in their last war against Rome, and had so nearly won. In 285 B.C. they had again invaded Etruria and massacred a Roman army. The Romans in fury dispatched another army which routed the invaders. The Romans now invaded the homeland of the Senones and mercilessly slaughtered the population, driving the remnants clean out of Italy.

Now the other tribes were massing. In 225 B.C. they crossed the Apennines with an army of 70,000 men. For the first time Rome was involved in a full scale war with the Celts. It was the beginning of the end for that proud people. Over the next 170 years Rome systematically massacred the Celts in northern Italy, Spain and France. It can be said without fear of contradiction that while the Romans were establishing their empire more Celts died than all the other peoples of the empire put together.

These wars are the best documented of all Roman history. We have not only the histories of the great Polybius but also Caesar's own account of his war against the Gallic Celts. There is also a very valuable description of the Celtic warrior given by Diodorus, a Greek writer from Sicily who lived in the first century B.C.

The archaeological record is vast and spreads from Turkey to Scotland. This part of the book examines the Celts not just in Italy but over the whole of western Europe from 500 B.C. to A.D. 100.

◀ *The Celtic tribes living in the Alps try to ambush Hannibal's army. They attack from the higher ground rolling boulders down on the Carthaginians as they are passing through a defile. The setting is the defile in the upper Durance valley ten kilometres south of Briancon.*

Warriors from the North

The Romans invade the Po Valley

To meet the Celtic attack in 225 B.C. Rome sent out two armies, each of 50,000 infantry and 3,200 cavalry. One was stationed at Rimini and the other in Tuscany. The Gauls forced a passage through the Apennines and attacked the legions in Tuscany. The army from Rimini arrived just in time to prevent a massacre. The Celts withdrew to the coast, with the army from Rimini hard on their heels. A third Roman army crossed over from Sardinia and the Celts were caught between the two Roman forces. Near Telamon, 140km north of Rome, 40,000 Celts fell

The origin of the Celts

The Celts came from southern Germany and spread across western Europe. By the 5th century B.C. they had over-run Austria, Switzerland, Belgium and Luxembourg, and parts of France, Spain and Britain.

In the following century the Celts invaded northern Italy. The first tribe to arrive was the Insubres who made their capital at Milan. The Boii, Lingones, Cenomani and other tribes followed and conquered most of the Po valley, finally driving the Etruscans back across the Apennines. The Senones arrived last. They pushed right down the Adriatic coast and settled around Ancona. (The Romans called the Celts "Gauls").

During the 4th and 3rd centuries B.C. more Celts settled in the Balkans and invaded Greece. They were driven back, but some of them crossed over into Asia and finally settled in Turkey.

The Greek and Roman historians

Most of our knowledge of the Celts unfortunately comes to us only through their enemies, the Greeks and Romans. Diodorus, the Sicilian, gives a vivid description of the warriors. He tells us of their colourful clothes, long moustaches and hair that was washed with lime to make it stand up like a horse's mane.

At first the Romans were terrified of these fair-haired giants. Later, when they realized that their discipline could always triumph over undisciplined valour, they grew scornful of the unruly barbarians. Livy's writing reflects this view. Contemptuous though the Romans may have been, under a good general the Celts made excellent soldiers. They made up nearly half of Hannibal's army, which for 15 years dominated the Roman legions. The Romans later recognized the Celts' worth and for centuries they filled the ranks of the legions.

▲ Part of the decoration of a cauldron found at Gundestrup, in Denmark. It shows Celtic horsemen, footsoldiers and trumpeters, 3rd-1st century B.C.

The warrior class

Most primitive societies had a warrior class: both the early Greeks and the Romans did. The Celts were no exception. Their warriors were drawn from what we would describe as the middle and upper class. The warrior class did the actual fighting: the free poor served as chariot drivers.

The Celt was a warrior in the heroic sense. Everything had to be larger than life. He lived for war. His glorification of bravery often led him to recklessness. Part of a warrior's ritual was to boast of his victories, and fighting between warriors was an important part of life.

fighting bravely to the end.

The threat of yet another invasion was over. The Romans swore that it was to be the last. The legions now invaded the Po valley itself. In the first campaign the Boii were brought to their knees. The following year (222 B.C.) the consul, Gaius Flaminius, who was later to be killed by Hannibal at the battle of Lake Trasimeno, crossed the Po and wiped out an army of the Insubres near Bergamo. The next year the legions captured Milan, the chief city of the Insubres. The Celts there surrendered unconditionally. The Romans settled colonies at Piacenza and Cremona.

Armour and weapons

Most Celts scorned the use of armour and before about 300 B.C. preferred to fight naked. Some Celtic tribes still fought naked at the battle of Telamon in 225 B.C.

The Celt was renowned as a swordsman but he also used javelins and spears. Two spears which were found at La Tène in Switzerland were nearly 2·5m long. His only protection was his large shield which was usually oval. The suggestion that the Celt wore heavy bracelets in battle has to be questioned, as it is hard to understand how they would stay on his arm whilst he wielded his sword.

Dionysius tells us that in battle the Celts whirled their swords above their heads, slashing the air from side to side, then struck downwards at their enemies as if chopping wood. It was this use of the sword that so terrified their enemies.

The Celts did not fight in a rabble as is so often supposed. They were organized in companies. This can be proved by their use of standards.

Headhunters

The Celt was a headhunter. In battle he would cut off the head of his fallen enemy and often hang it from his horse's neck. After battle he would display the severed head at the entrance to his temple. The severed head is a constant theme in Celtic art. At the battle of Beneventum in 214 B.C. the Roman general Gracchus had to order his army of freed slaves (presumably Celts) to stop collecting heads and get on with the fighting.

After a battle the Celts would often dedicate their enemies' weapons to the gods and throw them into a river or lake. The hundreds of weapons that have been dredged from the Lake of Neuchâtel at La Tène were such offerings. In fact the site at La Tène has revealed so many Celtic artifacts that its name has been given to the whole Celtic culture.

The chiefs

The chiefs and the wealthiest Celts often did wear armour particularly when they came into contact with the Greeks and Romans. They often adopted items of Greek or Roman armour. A pair of greaves were found in the chieftain's grave at Ciumesti.

Several graves have been found in Northern Italy which contain Etruscan armour and Celtic weapons. It is unlikely the graves are Celtic as there is one at S. Marino in Gattara about 50km from Bologna which contains not only an Etruscan helmet and greaves but also the handgrip attachments for a hoplite shield.

Before a battle the chiefs would ride out in front of the army clashing their weapons on their shields, proclaiming their great deeds and challenging the enemy to single combat.

Caesar describes the British as dressed in skins and decorated with woad, a blue dye. Some tattooed skin from a Scythian grave of this period suggests that the Britons were tattooed in blue.

▲ Representations of Celtic foot soldiers on a 4th century B.C. sword scabbard, from Halstatt in Austria.

▲ A Senones Chieftain c.300 B.C. Although chiefs regularly wore helmets and other armour the ordinary warriors at this time preferred to fight naked, like the two figures in the background.

Celtic Hill Forts

▲ *A reconstruction of the* oppidum *at Entremont seen from the north. The battlements are shown made of wood but they might well have been made of stone or brick. The fortress was captured by the Romans in 123 B.C.*

▲ *Entremont: part of the north wall and a tower. The wall, which was 2m thick, was built of rough-cut stones. The solid tower is 8m wide. It was probably surmounted by a hollow tower.*

▼ *Nages: a gate from the 2nd and 3rd stages of development of the fort. This tower also has a solid base.*

▼ *Nages: a plan of the tower and wall above showing its structure.*

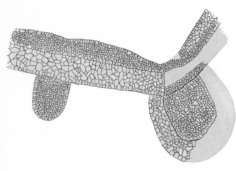

Early hill forts

A hill fort is the name given to any fortified hilltop settlement. Normally it consisted of a village or refuge defended by ramparts and ditches, occupying either the whole or part of a hilltop. Its area might vary from one to 350 hectares. Thousands of hill forts have been discovered in western Europe.

Hill forts were common to all ancient European peoples. Originally, most were defended by palisades. But they were insufficient, and were often replaced by a ditch and earthen rampart with a vertical outer side faced with timber. These timber-faced ramparts were gradually replaced by better types of rampart.

Stone and brick fortifications

In the south, in the 6th to 5th century B.C., the early Celts, influenced by the Greeks, started facing their ramparts with stone or clay bricks. In the south of France several Celtic fortresses have been discovered built entirely of stone. They date from the 3rd century B.C. and are based on the Greek fortifications at nearby Marseilles. The most famous is at Entremont.

The fortress at Entremont

This triangular fortress is on a high ridge overlooking Aix-en-Provence. Two sides have a steep approach and were probably defended by a simple wall. The north side has a flat approach. Here part of the wall has been excavated. It is about 2.5m thick and is reinforced by towers at 19m intervals. Only the lower parts survive; built of rough-cut stones of varying size and shape, laid in irregular courses (illustration, left). The towers were filled with rubble to withstand battering rams. As they are based on Greek models, it seems certain they are real towers, not just bastions. If so, they would have been topped with battlements of stone, brick or wood.

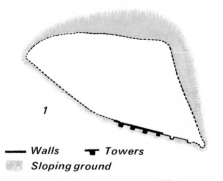

— Walls   ⊤ Towers
░ Sloping ground

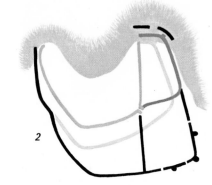

▲ *Plans of hill forts in southern France.*
1. Entremont. 2. Nages.
The successive developments of Nages are shown by darker grey. The latest fortifications are black.

The *oppidum* at Nages

The more important forts such as the one at Entremont were called *oppida* (singular *oppidum*) by the Romans.

Another such *oppidum* is the hill fort at Nages. This lies to the west of the Rhône near Nîmes and guards the route to Spain. Hannibal would have had to march past it on his route to Italy. It occupies part of a hilltop. It has walls on three sides. The fourth side is defended by a steep hillside. The side which is open to the rest of the hilltop is defended by a wall reinforced with towers, as at Entremont. This fort is particularly interesting as it shows four successive stages of development (see plan above).

Murus Gallicus

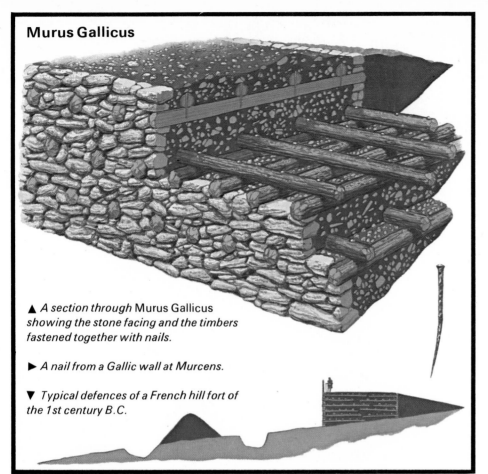

▲ *A section through* Murus Gallicus *showing the stone facing and the timbers fastened together with nails.*

▶ *A nail from a Gallic wall at Murcens.*

▼ *Typical defences of a French hill fort of the 1st century B.C.*

Hill fort plans

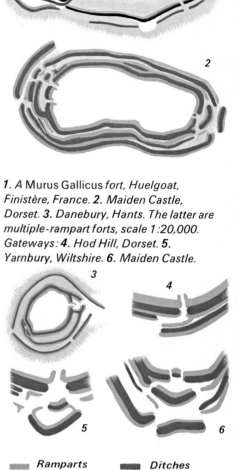

1. A Murus Gallicus *fort, Huelgoat, Finistère, France.* **2.** *Maiden Castle, Dorset.* **3.** *Danebury, Hants. The latter are multiple-rampart forts, scale 1:20,000. Gateways:* **4.** *Hod Hill, Dorset.* **5.** *Yarnbury, Wiltshire.* **6.** *Maiden Castle.*

Ramparts	Ditches
Murus Gallicus	Sloping ground

Murus Gallicus

In central and northern France the earlier ramparts were replaced by a type of structure described by Julius Caesar, who calls it simply Gallic wall (*Murus Gallicus*). This type of wall is built with stone facing at the front and back. The centre is filled with soil or rubble and laced with timbers. These were built into the stone wall at the front and the back.

The walls at Huelgoat, Finistère (see the illustration above) were almost 4m high. They would have been surmounted with battlements.

Caesar was impressed by this type of walling, as the stone facing prevented the wood being burnt, and the soil and timber fill prevented the wall from being battered down. From an external examination, Caesar's engineers could not have known that the walls also had timbers laid lengthways. They were nailed to the cross beams. These details have been revealed by excavations in France.

The thickness and composition of the walls vary considerably. Some have no stone facing on the inside. In front of the wall there were usually one or two lines of ditches. Timber-laced ramparts with stone facing of this period are often found in Britain. They are similar to *Murus Gallicus*, but not as sound.

Sloped and multiple ramparts

In Britain many timber-faced ramparts began to be replaced in the 3rd century B.C. Ditches were deepened and the ramparts sloped to form a steep unbroken incline. From about 100 B.C. many southern British hill forts increased their defences by adding more ditches and ramparts outside their original lines. The entrance to these forts was very complex. This was to stop the enemy charging the gates.

▼ *A reconstruction of the multiple-rampart hill fort of Danebury, in its last stage of development at the time of the Roman invasion in A.D. 43.*

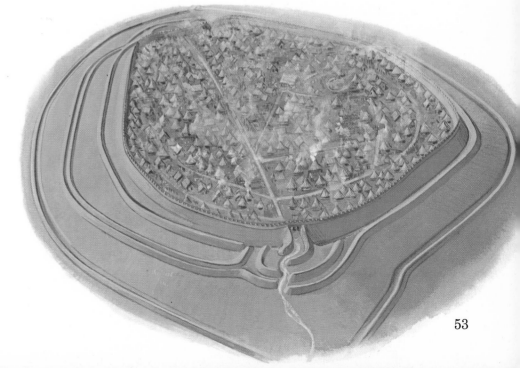

53

Celtic Chariots

The saviour arrives

Hannibal arrived in the autumn of 218 B.C. The mountains had taken a terrible toll. In crossing the Alps he had lost nearly half his army: of his original 46,000, only 26,000 men survived.

The Insubres, still smarting from their defeats by the Romans, welcomed the saviour with open arms.

The only Roman forces in the Po valley were Scipio's original legions which had been sent into the area earlier in the summer. Scipio had arrived just in time to take over the command. Sempronius, with another army, was at Lilybaeum in Sicily,

▲ A coin from the time of Caesar, showing a Celtic chariot.

▶ A grave-stone from Padua in northern Italy, showing a Celtic chariot with a double semi-circular side, c.300 B.C.

▼ 1 and 2. A yoke and wheel from La Tène in Switzerland, c.200 B.C. 3-15. Metal parts of chariots from French chariot burials. 3, 4 and 11. Articulated harness attachments 5. Hub-cap with linchpin. 7. Felloe joint. 8 and 9. Bronze decorations. 10. Horse-bit. 12 and 15. Linchpins. 13. Rein-guide (terret). 6 and 14. Eye bolts, of uncertain purpose.

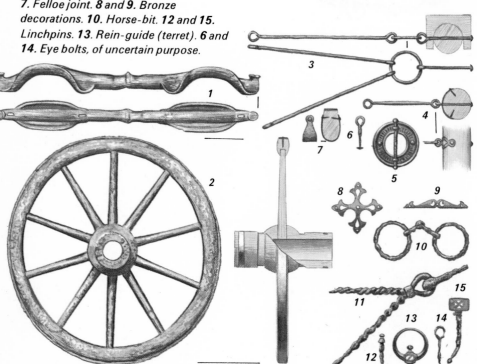

The last chariots

Polybius, in his account of the events leading up to the battle of Telamon, 225 B.C. says that the Gallic army had 20,000 cavalry and chariots. This is the last reference to chariots being used in warfare on the European mainland. They are not encountered again until Caesar invades Britain in 55 B.C.

Diodorus tells us that chariots were drawn by two horses and carried a driver and a warrior. In battle the warrior threw javelins from his chariot and then descended and fought on foot. Caesar's account of the British chariots is very similar, but he adds one very important detail: chariots were used against cavalry. One could not fight against infantry in this way except in skirmishes.

Caesar expresses great admiration for the charioteers' skill. He describes warriors running along the chariot pole and standing on the yoke above the horses' shoulders.

waiting to go into Africa. He now marched north.

Scipio, advancing along the north bank of the Po with his cavalry, fell straight into an ambush. Although wounded, he managed to disengage his troops and retreat. He crossed the Po and took up a defensive position on the east bank of the Trebbia in the foothills of the Apennines near Piacenza. Here he waited for his colleague. Hannibal also crossed the Po and advanced to within a few kilometres of the Romans. Sempronius arrived a few days later.

Hannibal was well aware of Sempronius' intemperate character, and laid his plans accordingly.

Skirmishes regularly took place between the camps. The Carthaginian deliberately allowed the Romans to get the better of his men. It was all Sempronius needed. He could not wait to start fighting.

Several streams flowed across the plain that separated the two armies. That night Hannibal dispatched his brother Mago with 1,000 cavalry and as many infantry to hide in the foothills along the bed of one of these streams.

At dawn he sent out his Numidian horsemen to harass the Roman camp. He then ordered his whole army to breakfast, and stand by their arms.

▲ *Etruscan chariot horses from Tarquinii, showing the method of harnessing the yoke: probably very similar to the Celtic method.*

▼ *A reconstruction of a chariot showing the long box with its double semi-circular sides. To prevent the box coming apart from the wheels the trace reins are attached to the axle. The towing pole is attached to the box and axle.*

Chariot graves

Several chariot graves have been found in France. Sadly, some chariots appear to have been dismantled before burial.

Many metal parts of chariots have been preserved in these graves. Among them are articulated harnessings (left **3**, **4**, **11**) which must have been used for the attachment of trace reins. (The length of the bolt on these suggests they were attached to the axle. This is certainly the position in which they were found in the grave.)

The series of rings that were found level with the horse's chest may have been fastened to the girth strap to guide the trace reins. The graves contain many other items: linchpins for securing the wheels (**12**, **15**) and rein guides (terrets) which were attached to the yoke (**13**).

A very well preserved yoke (**1**), and wheel complete with iron tyre (**2**), were dredged from the lake at La Tène.

A reconstruction of the Celtic chariot

Until recently we had to rely on coins to give us some idea of the form of Celtic chariots. These coins show vehicles with what appear to be two semi-circular sides. A few years ago a grave-stone was found in northern Italy which shows that the two semi-circular pieces are in fact only one side. This is supported by the archaeological evidence. In French chariot burials the space between the wheels is little over a metre, far less than in the Cypriot chariots, where driver and warrior stood side by side. A Celtic warrior must therefore have stood behind his driver. The long chariot box needed for this accounts for the double sides and for how a warrior could be laid lengthways in his chariot, as he was in the French burials.

Cavalry, Trumpets and Standards

A shattering defeat

Sempronius saw the Numidians coming and ordered out his cavalry. He followed up with his javelineers and finally ordered out his whole army. The Numidians retreated and the Romans followed. Down they plunged into the icy waters of the Trebbia which had been swollen by rain during the night. Snow was blowing in the wind as they stumbled over the shingle, the water dragging at their legs. They plunged down again and again into the troughs of the river. At last, soaked and shivering, the legionaries clambered up the far bank.

▲ *A Celtic horseman with round spined shield, from the victory monument of Aemilius Paullus at Delphi, 168 B.C.*

Were Celtic horsemen really cavalry?

It has been suggested that the Celts had no true cavalry, and that they dismounted and fought on foot. At the battle of Cannae the Celts, Spaniards and Romans certainly did this, but it may have been because of the cramped space in which they were fighting. The comment of Hannibal, recorded by Livy, seems to contradict this. When he was told that Paullus had ordered his cavalry to dismount, Hannibal said that he might as well have delivered them up in chains. This implies that dismounted cavalry were useless. In fact it is hard to imagine large numbers of cavalry dismounting to fight. Certainly the Romans did not normally do this or Polybius' comments about their adopting the Greek spear, which did not waver in the charge, would have no meaning.

Cavalry equipment

Many Celtic horse-bits have been found. They are usually of the snaffle type. The sculpture (left) shows a horseman serving with the Macedonian forces at the battle of Pydna (168 B.C.). The round shield, which is certainly neither Roman nor Greek, must be a Celtic cavalry shield.

The sculpture on the right shows a Celt riding over a fallen Greek. The riderless horse shows the type of saddle in use among the Greeks at this time. The Celts used the same type of saddle as the later Romans. This saddle with pommels at each corner appears on the Gundestrup cauldron (see below). This cauldron also shows the discs that were used to decorate Celtic horses. Some of these, made of silver, have been found in northern Italy.

◀ *Third century Celtic cavalrymen.*

▼ *A Celtic horseman from the Gundestrup cauldron. The horse has a four pommelled saddle, and decorated harness discs. 3rd-1st century B.C.*

Hannibal now ordered out his forces. His infantry was in the centre and the cavalry on the wings. The Numidians had scattered, and the Romans recalled their cavalry and javelineers. The legions now advanced at a slow march with the light-armed out ahead and the cavalry on either wing.

The result of the battle could never really have been in doubt. The Romans were soaking wet and shivering and had not even had breakfast. The legionaries threw their *pila* and rushed in with swords. The Carthaginian cavalry charged and stripped the flanks of the legions bare. Now the African pikemen, who had been held back, rushed past their own troops and attacked the Roman flanks. The legionaries fought bravely but they were completely routed. When Mago led his two thousand troops out of their hiding place and attacked the Roman rear the legions were completely surrounded. Some of the Romans managed to break through the Carthaginian line. Others turned and ran for the river. The victorious Carthaginian cavalry was hard on their heels. Many Romans died as they tried to cross the river. Others, weakened by hunger and wounds, were washed away.

▲ A sculpture showing a Greek and Celtic horseman, c.200 B.C.

▶ 1. Silver harness disc from northern Italy. 2. Horse-bit, c.400 B.C. 3. Horse-bit, c.50 B.C. 4. British horse-bit.

Trumpets and standards

The commonest trumpet used by the Celts was the *carnyx*. This was long, with a mouth in the form of an animal's head. These are shown on the Gundestrup cauldron (p.50) and on the arch of Orange in southern France (see right). The horn was also used in northern Italy. The sculpture on the right shows a Celtic horn blower and a standard bearer. The standard bearer has a Negau helmet and a distinctively shaped shield. A similar shield is to be seen on the tombstone of a Roman auxiliary standard bearer from Hadrian's Wall. Flags and animal standards were also used (see arch of Orange). The strange spearheads with shapes cut out were probably from standards.

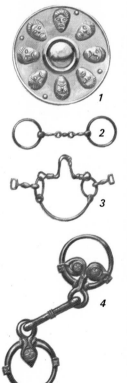

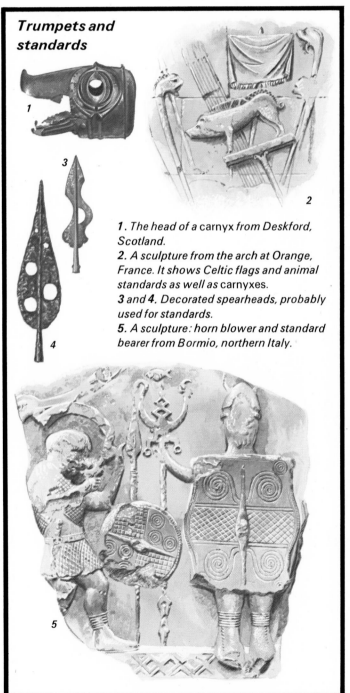

Trumpets and standards

1. The head of a carnyx from Deskford, Scotland.
2. A sculpture from the arch at Orange, France. It shows Celtic flags and animal standards as well as carnyxes.
3 and 4. Decorated spearheads, probably used for standards.
5. A sculpture: horn blower and standard bearer from Bormio, northern Italy.

Swords and Spears

During the night Scipio and those who had escaped to the camp fled to Piacenza. The Romans had lost more than 20,000 men in the battle. All the Celts now joined Hannibal. The Carthaginians could not follow up their victory because of a terrible snow-storm that followed. Only one elephant survived the following winter, and many of the horses died.

At Rome the winter was spent in feverish preparations. Eleven new legions were enrolled (100,000 men) and placed under the command of the new consuls. Flaminius, the leader of the people's party

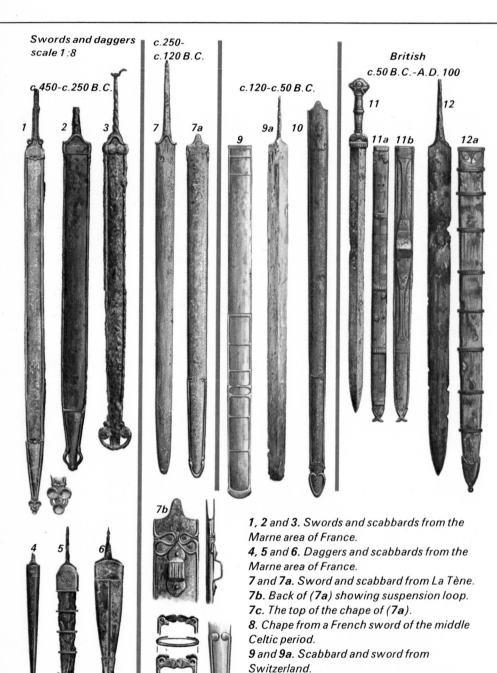

Swords and daggers scale 1:8

c.250-c.120 B.C.

c.450-c.250 B.C.

c.120-c.50 B.C.

British c.50 B.C.-A.D. 100

1, 2 and 3. Swords and scabbards from the Marne area of France.
4, 5 and 6. Daggers and scabbards from the Marne area of France.
7 and 7a. Sword and scabbard from La Tène.
7b. Back of (7a) showing suspension loop.
7c. The top of the chape of (7a).
8. Chape from a French sword of the middle Celtic period.
9 and 9a. Scabbard and sword from Switzerland.
10. Scabbard from the Thames.
11, 11b. Sword, and front and back of scabbard from Cumberland.
12, 12a. Sword and scabbard from Yorkshire.

The long sword of the Celts

The picture of the great Celtic slashing swords, given by ancient authors, is not entirely true. It really applies only to the late 3rd-1st century B.C.

Polybius says that the Romans used to take the first blow of the Celtic sword on the rim of their shield and that the swords bent double. This may have happened, but Celtic swords were better than this. The author has seen a 2,000 year old sword from the lake at La Tène bend almost double, then spring back.

Early swords (c.450-c.250 B.C.)

Most early swords have pointed blades between 55cm and 65cm in length. Sword (1) is exceptional. It has a blade 80cm long. Daggers with blades 25-30cm long are common. The main characteristic of these early weapons is their pronounced chape (foot of the sheath).

The middle period (c.250-c.120 B.C.)

During this period blades became round-ended, and gradually increased in length until blades of 75-80cm were common. Although the early chape forms continued in the east, in western Europe the chape followed more closely the contour of the sword. The most typical is the La Tène sword from Switzerland (7).

The late period (c.120-c.50 B.C.)

The average length of blade now increased to over 80cm. Some examples are as long as 90cm. Although pointed swords existed, the predominant type was the flat-ended sword (9). The scabbard (10) is British. Its chape is derived from the La Tène type but the length suggests the late period.

British swords (c.50 B.C.-A.D.100)

Sword blades have become pointed and shorter, 55-57cm. (11) is typical, with its small twin-footed chape.

(the man who had slaughtered the Insubres six years before) took up his position at Arezzo in northern Tuscany, with two legions. His colleague, Geminus, was stationed at Rimini, also with two legions. Of the other seven legions, two were sent to Spain, two to Sicily, one to Sardinia and two remained in reserve at Rome.

During the winter Hannibal had studied the character of the two consuls and knew that Flaminius was the more likely to be tempted. As soon as the weather permitted, the Carthaginian forced a passage through the Apennines. It had been an appalling winter and the valley of the Arno was flooded. Hoping to surprise Flaminius, Hannibal decided to cross the flooded valley rather than skirt it. For three days and nights the army struggled through the marshes. Most of the pack animals which had survived the Alpine crossing died in the mud. Hannibal rode the only surviving elephant. He had caught a disease in his eye and, because of the desperate situation of the army, there was no time to stop and treat it. By the time they were out of the marshes it was too late. The disease was too far advanced and one eye had to be removed.

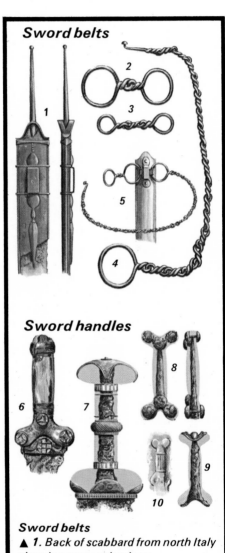

Sword belts

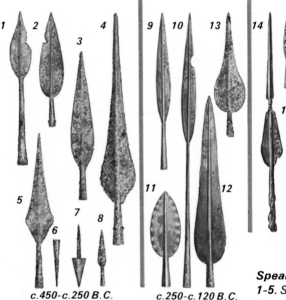

c.450-c.250 B.C.   c.250-c.120 B.C.

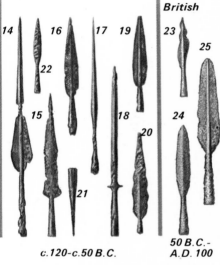

British

c.120-c.50 B.C.   50 B.C.-A.D. 100

Sword belts
▲ 1. Back of scabbard from north Italy showing suspension loop.
2, 3 and 4. Parts of sword chains (or belts).
5. Method of attaching sword.
Sword handles
6. From Thorpe, Bridlington, Yorkshire.
7. From Hod Hill, Dorset.
8. From the Marne valley, France.
9. From Hallstatt, Austria.
10. Sculpture from Pergamon, Turkey.

Sword belts
Swords are often found with rings and pieces of chain (see 2, 3, 4, in the box). These are parts of the belt. The long chain (4), usually about 50-60cm long, forms the back part of the belt. The ring end has a strap attached which passes through the loop on the scabbard and is attached to the double ring (2) or piece of chain (3) to complete the belt. The sword is worn on the right. More often two rings were strapped to the scabbard loop, and a leather belt replaced the chain using fasteners.

Sword handles
The traditional sword handle was in the form of an elongated X. Sometimes on ceremonial swords this was made in the form of a man with his arms raised. The handle (6), although late, still echoes the traditional form. Late types (7) were often influenced by Roman models. Handles were probably made of wood and have thus nearly always disappeared.

Spears and javelins. Scale 1:8.
1-5. Spear heads. 6, 7. Spear butts. 8. Javelin head. 2, 5, 6. From the Marne area, France. 4. From north Italy. 1, 3, 7, 8. Origin unknown. 9-12. Spear heads from La Tène. 13. Spear head from the Marne area. 14-20. Spear heads. 21. Spear butt. 22. Javelin head. 14-22. From Alesia, France. 23. Javelin head, southern England. 24, 25. Spear heads, Scotland.

Spears
Two complete spears were discovered at La Tène. These were nearly 2.5m long. Spearheads came in a great variety of shapes. Some examples of these are shown above. The typically Celtic types are those which curve inwards between the widest point and the tip (1, 4, 5, 12, 13, 14). Some are as long as 50cm whilst others, probably for javelins, are as short as 10cm. Spear butts come in both socketed and tanged types. Wherever the Celts came up against the Romans they adopted the socketed type of Roman javelin (*pilum*). Examples of these have been found at many Celtic sites in southern Europe.

Generals and Tactics

A trap is sprung

As soon as the army had rested they advanced on Arezzo where Flaminius was encamped. It was the Roman plan that whichever way Hannibal advanced the consul there would wait for his colleague to join him, so that they could combine forces as they had done against the Gauls eight years before.

With this knowledge Hannibal advanced to the very walls of Arezzo, ravaging the country and burning the crops. When Flaminius refused to come out Hannibal by-passed him and advanced south towards Rome, burning everything. It was too much

▲ *A statue of a general in full dress panoply found at the island of Rhodes. Probably 3rd century B.C.*

▼ *Shoulder guards from cuirasses of the type shown above.*

The commanding officer

The qualities necessary to make a good general are given to us by Onasander, a Greek philosopher of the first century A.D. He tells us that a general should have the following virtues: self-control, temperance, vigilance and frugality. He should be free from greed, hardened to labour, and a good speaker, for he must be able to encourage his troops. Onasander also suggests that he should be a father, and middle-aged. This last is a very conservative view: the three great generals of antiquity, Alexander, Hannibal and Scipio, all achieved their greatest victories in their youth.

Both Polybius and Onasander insist that a general's duty is to direct his troops and not to become involved in the fighting. If he is involved he cannot see the overall effect of his strategy.

Polybius goes further. He says that a general who leads his troops into battle is seen by them all but sees none of them. Here is a strong criticism of Alexander who always led his cavalry. The greatest danger is that he might be killed, with a demoralizing effect on his troops.

Generals must remain apart from their troops, giving their orders down the chain of command. Only in the most dire circumstances should a general involve himself directly, and only when the effect might encourage disheartened troops.

The price of failure

All ancient states prosecuted unsuccessful generals. Greeks and Romans fined commanders who failed to achieve the expected standards. The Greeks banished many and even stoned some to death. But none treated their defeated officers as brutally as the Carthaginians. Beaten generals were regularly crucified, sometimes even by their own troops. The families of defeated generals were often disgraced with them.

The duties of the general

In brief, a general's duties were to supervize and understand all the activities of the army. He must make sure that his troops were smart and well drilled. He had to ensure that every man knew his place in the battle line-up. The soldier had to be familiar with the men next to him in both rank and file, for only amongst his friends would a man fight his best. A general should never allow his foragers too much freedom as they were easy prey for the enemy cavalry.

Religion and morale

A general must always sacrifice and make sure that the omens were favourable before setting out on a march or offering battle. He must also sacrifice in thanksgiving after an engagement. It was his duty to make sure that all the bodies were buried after a battle, as the soldiers would feel that they too might be left unburied and this would undermine their morale. However, Polybius says the most important duty of a general was to understand the strengths and weaknesses of his opponent. Hannibal distinguished himself at this. Again and again he exploited the faults of Roman generals.

Carthaginian tactics

The Carthaginians were probably the greatest exponents of the use of mercenary troops. In spite of the contempt that Greek and Roman authors have for the Carthaginian armies, these hired soldiers put up a better show against Rome than any of her opponents. They very nearly won. In tactics, the Carthaginians excelled: the Romans generally referred to Carthaginian tactics as "Punic treachery". They loved ambushes. Hannibal and his brother Hasdrubal ambushed six Roman generals. When their forces lined up, part of their troops were always screened from the enemy.

for Flaminius. He broke camp and followed.

The route south follows a broad valley about 35km long. At the end of the valley is a lake surrounded on three sides by hills. Here the road forks and one half follows the north edge of the lake heading for Perugia. At the point where the road forks a spur juts out from the northern hills to the water's edge. Further along the northern shore the hills again advance to the water's edge to form a plain.

Hannibal timed his march to arrive at the lake late in the afternoon. He turned along the water's edge, crossed the plain and camped on the hillside.

Flaminius reached the corner of the lake as dusk was falling and encamped for the night. The following morning the Romans broke camp and again set out in pursuit. They rounded the spur and entered the plain. Mist was rising from the lake and drifting up the hills, shrouding the fifty thousand men formed up in battle order along the hillsides. As soon as the Roman rearguard had passed the spur the order was given. Suddenly the whole hillside came to life, as with a mighty roar mingled with blaring of trumpets, Celts, Africans and Spaniards thundered down on the unsuspecting legionaries.

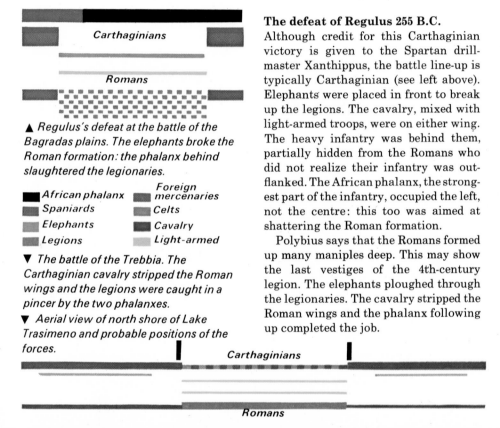

▲ Regulus's defeat at the battle of the Bagradas plains. The elephants broke the Roman formation: the phalanx behind slaughtered the legionaries.

African phalanx	Foreign mercenaries
Spaniards	Celts
Elephants	Cavalry
Legions	Light-armed

▼ The battle of the Trebbia. The Carthaginian cavalry stripped the Roman wings and the legions were caught in a pincer by the two phalanxes.

▼ Aerial view of north shore of Lake Trasimeno and probable positions of the forces.

The defeat of Regulus 255 B.C.

Although credit for this Carthaginian victory is given to the Spartan drill-master Xanthippus, the battle line-up is typically Carthaginian (see left above). Elephants were placed in front to break up the legions. The cavalry, mixed with light-armed troops, were on either wing. The heavy infantry was behind them, partially hidden from the Romans who did not realize their infantry was out-flanked. The African phalanx, the strong-est part of the infantry, occupied the left, not the centre: this too was aimed at shattering the Roman formation.

Polybius says that the Romans formed up many maniples deep. This may show the last vestiges of the 4th-century legion. The elephants ploughed through the legionaries. The cavalry stripped the Roman wings and the phalanx following up completed the job.

The battle of the Trebbia

Hannibal's formation at the Trebbia is almost identical to the one he used at Cannae (see p.71). He placed his Spanish and Celtic swordsmen in the centre. On the wings he placed his cavalry with the elephants in front. Behind, screened from the Romans, he placed his phalanx drawn up in two columns. The legions charged in the centre. The Punic cavalry and elephants stripped the Roman wings. The phalanx ran forward, faced inward and charged the Roman flanks.

The battle of Lake Trasimeno

Trasimeno is a classic ambush. Unfortunately Polybius appears to have got his topography wrong. The north-west shore of Lake Trasimeno has considerably changed since Roman times due to a combination of drainage and silting up, but it still does not fit Polybius' description. Hannibal drew up his troops by night, along the tree-covered hillsides above the lake. The following morning the Romans followed. Mist was rising from the lake. They were caught unawares and driven into the lake.

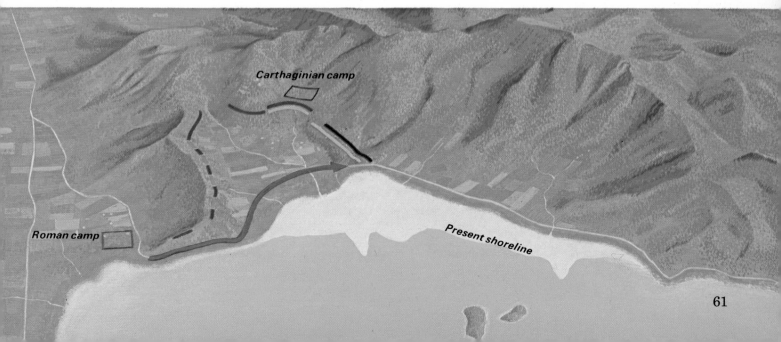

Carthaginian camp

Roman camp

Present shoreline

Celtic Helmets

The Insubres are avenged

The legionaries had no time to form up in battle order, but fought where they stood. Gradually they were driven back to the water's edge where they stumbled in the reeds and slime amidst the croaking frogs. Here they were cut to pieces by the cavalry. Some tried to swim to safety, but, weighed down by their armour, were drowned.

Flaminius himself, fighting bravely, was surrounded and killed by the Insubres who sought vengeance for his treatment of them five years before. The complete Roman army of 20,000 men was either

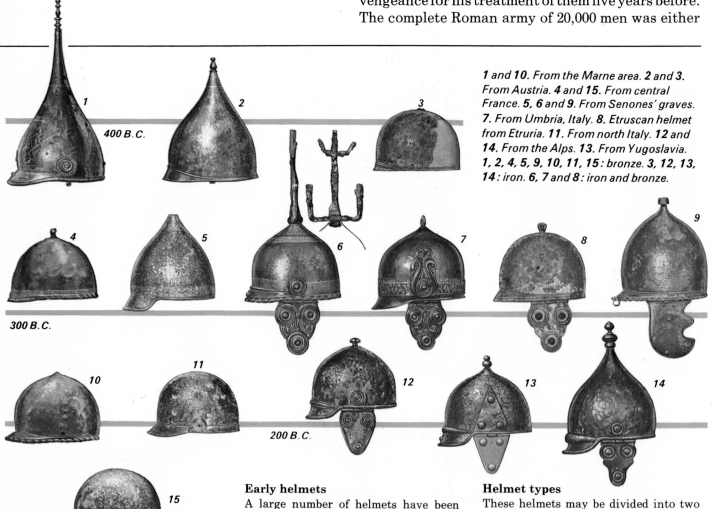

1 and *10*. From the Marne area. *2* and *3*. From Austria. *4* and *15*. From central France. *5*, *6* and *9*. From Senones' graves. *7*. From Umbria, Italy. *8*. Etruscan helmet from Etruria. *11*. From north Italy. *12* and *14*. From the Alps. *13*. From Yugoslavia. *1, 2, 4, 5, 9, 10, 11, 15*: bronze. *3, 12, 13, 14*: iron. *6, 7* and *8*: iron and bronze.

400 B.C.

300 B.C.

200 B.C.

100 B.C.

▲ *16* and *17*. From Switzerland. Both are iron, and (*16*) was the forerunner of the 1st century A.D. Roman legionary helmets.

Early helmets

A large number of helmets have been discovered in the Senones' region of Italy, all with a back peak to protect the neck. They are generally called Montefortino, after the burial ground where they were first found. These can be traced to a type of helmet used in France and Austria in the later 5th century (**1, 2**).

Numbers (**5**), (**6**) and (**9**) are from Senones' graves, and date to before 282 B.C. when these Celts were driven out by the Romans. Cheek-pieces are nearly always of the triple-disc type (**6**). Their similarity to the triple-disc breastplates (p.24) suggests Samnite origin. In the 3rd century, this cheek-piece degenerated into a triangular one with three bosses.

Helmet types

These helmets may be divided into two types: those with a top knot and those with a round cap (**3, 11, 15**). The top knot type is by far the most common. The round capped type became more popular in the 1st century B.C. but its origin is much earlier. An example was found in the Senones' graves, and (**3**) which is from Halstatt, may be as early as 400 B.C. The Montefortino types of helmet were made of iron or bronze, or both.

These helmets were adopted by the Italians. Only a few examples have been found with triple-disc cheek-pieces at non-Celtic sites (**8**). Helmets with scalloped cheek-pieces, (**9**), were standard for the Roman army, and in use until early in the 1st century A.D.

killed or captured. In an attempt to alienate Rome's allies, Hannibal released all the non-Roman prisoners and sent them home telling them that his fight was with Rome and not with them. He had done the same after the battle at the Trebbia.

The news of Sempronius' defeat the year before had been softened because conflicting reports had been received and it was only later that the full extent of the disaster was realized. This time there could be no doubt. The city *praetor* called together the people in the forum and told them, "We have been defeated in a great battle". But there was more to come.

The other consul had received Flaminius' call and was advancing to join him. He sent ahead his entire cavalry, 4,000 strong. Unaware of the disaster that had overtaken Flaminius they advanced southwards in haste, and met a similar fate.

The Etruscans' spirit had long since been broken and they did not join Hannibal as he had hoped. The Carthaginian decided that he stood a far better chance in the south where the Samnites still remembered their ancient greatness. So he crossed to the Adriatic coast and descended on Apulia.

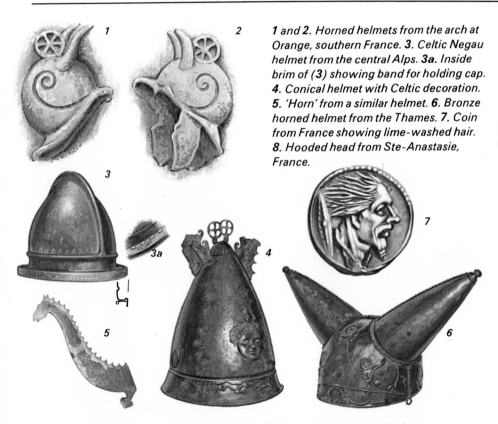

1 and 2. Horned helmets from the arch at Orange, southern France. 3. Celtic Negau helmet from the central Alps. 3a. Inside brim of (3) showing band for holding cap. 4. Conical helmet with Celtic decoration. 5. 'Horn' from a similar helmet. 6. Bronze horned helmet from the Thames. 7. Coin from France showing lime-washed hair. 8. Hooded head from Ste-Anastasie, France.

Late Celtic helmets

In the 1st century B.C. two new types appear (**16, 17**). Both are iron. Number 16 was the prototype for the standard Roman helmet in the 1st century A.D. Although cheek-pieces are now of the scalloped type some still have bosses echoing the triple-disc cheek-pieces (see below). In fact these discs still appear on Roman helmets in the 1st century A.D.

▲ Later Celtic cheek-pieces with bosses.
1. Yugoslavia. 2. Alesia.

Winged and horned helmets

Some helmets have a sort of wing design on the side (see left, **7, 13**). This type seems to have originated in Italy It may have been inspired by the wings on Samnite helmets. The type became popular in the Balkans in the 3rd-2nd century B.C. and it also appears on the victory frieze from Pergamon in Turkey. An example, though it may be an import, has also been found in France.

Horned helmets are shown on the arch at Orange (above, **1, 2**). These are probably ceremonial helmets. Several helmets with horn like attachments cut out of thin bronze sheet (**4, 5**) have been found in Italy. A superb example of a horned ceremonial helmet has been found in the River Thames at Waterloo Bridge (**6**).

Adopted helmets

Some 4th century B.C. Celtic graves have been discovered in northern Italy, containing Etruscan Negau helmets. That the Celts adopted the Negau helmet is proved by several examples of a Celtic form of Negau helmet found in the central Alpine area (**3**).

Helmets of Greek/Italian conical type with Celtic decoration, such as (**4**) have also been found. The wheel decoration on top is almost identical to those shown on the arch at Orange.

Lime-washed hair

Even in northern Italy, where helmet finds are common, the vast majority of Celts wore no armour. Diodorus tells us that these warriors lime washed their hair and then combed it back from the forehead to the nape of the neck so that it looked like a horse's mane. Several coins, such as (**7**) on the left, show this style. This attempt to make the hair stand up like an angry animal is very primitive and may point to the origin of horsehair crests on helmets.

Hoods

Some statues from southern France west of the Rhône, show extraordinary headgear like a hood with a crest on it (see above). These may be pre-Celtic and do show a great similarity to hoods shown on the Osuna reliefs from Spain (p.42).

Celtic Body Armour

At Rome, the Senate named Quintus Fabius Maximus dictator. Fabius knew that Hannibal, like Pyrrhus, had one weakness: manpower. To allow the Romans time to rebuild their forces, Fabius' policy was to whittle down Hannibal's army by capturing stragglers, and to deny Hannibal any chance of a brilliant victory by avoiding full scale battle.

Fabius advanced into Apulia with four legions. When the Romans refused to fight, Hannibal marched across Italy looting and burning to illustrate to Rome's allies how incapable the Romans were of

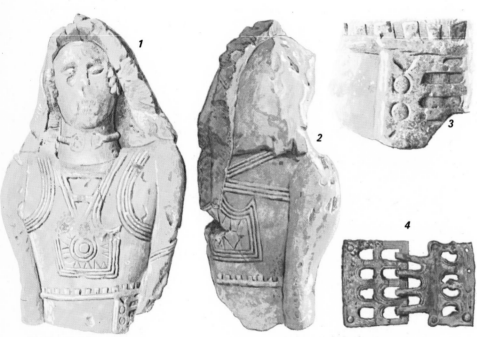

◀ **1** and **2**. Front and back views of a statue of a warrior from Grézan, near Nîmes, south of France. This statue may be as early as the 4th century B.C. **3**. Detail of the belt fastener of the warrior of Grézan. **4**. A belt fastener of the type worn by the Grézan warrior (this is not a Celtic type).

Early Celtic armour

The use of body armour among the Celts was probably very rare. Apart from a few bronze discs, which could be chest armour but are more likely to be harness decorations for horses, there is nothing from the early period (450-250 B.C.).

The warrior of Grézan

The 4th-3rd century statue from Grézan in the south of France (**1, 2, 3,** above) shows a warrior wearing what appears to be either a square front and back plate which is strapped on, or a complete cuirass decorated in this form.

This statue cannot be considered as typically Celtic: it may not be Celtic at all. The hood type helmet, like those from Ste-Anastasie (see p.63) probably originated among the Iberians and not the Celts. Therefore parallels should be looked for in Spain, not France. The belt fastener which is common to the whole of southern France and Corsica is a pre-Celtic type.

The invention of mail

Around 300 B.C. mail was invented. In spite of the Celtic distaste for armour most of the evidence points to the Celts as the inventor of mail, the most successful form of armour. Strabo refers to mail as Celtic. The earliest remains are from Celtic graves and the Celts are the great iron-workers of the ancient world. Several statues of warriors from southern France which have been thought to show pigskin or leather cuirasses should be regarded as depicting mail.

The use of mail, which was very expensive to make, was probably restricted to the aristocracy.

The various statues of mailed warriors from southern France and northern Italy show two types of cuirass: one with a cape that hangs over the shoulders (see 1, p.65) and one that was cut like a Greek linen cuirass with no overhang at the shoulders (see **4, 5**). The first is probably the truly Celtic type.

▲ Statue of a late Celtic warrior from Vachères, south of France. He wears a Romano-Celtic mail shirt.

▶ Insubres chief, c.200 B.C.

defending them. His tactics worked brilliantly and, within a matter of weeks, allies and Romans alike were desperately badgering the dictator to stop him.

When the six months of Fabius' dictatorship were up the people demanded action. They named as consuls Lucius Aemilius Paullus, an able soldier, and the less experienced Caius Terentius Varro. Their commission was simply to defeat Hannibal.

Hannibal now took up his position at the south end of the plain of Foggia near the village of Cannae: a name that was to resound through history as the site of Rome's greatest defeat.

1. Sculpture of mail shirt from Entremont, south France. 2. Detail of fastener from similar statue. 3. Mail with fastener from Ciumesti, Romania. A, B, C. The 3 types of ring used in the Ciumesti mail, actual size. D. Section of mail.
▼ 4. Sculptured mail shirt from Pergamon, Turkey. 5. Mailed statuette from north Italy. 6-8. Belt fasteners.

The mail shirt from Ciumesti
Pieces of a mail shirt were discovered in a 3rd-century grave at Ciumesti in Romania. There appear to be parts of two different cuirasses as one of them (3, left) is made up of alternate rows of punched (A) and butted (B) rings.

Another piece has riveted rings instead of butted ones. This is much stronger. These rings are 7mm in diameter. It is possible that the shirt with butted rings was for ceremonial purposes only. Attached to the butted mail is a bronze fastener, decorated with rosettes, for the shoulder pieces. The section (D) shows that one end was riveted to the mail of one shoulder piece, the centre rosette was purely decorative, and the far end must have hooked behind a similar rosette on the other shoulder piece.

This must be from a cuirass with overhanging shoulders, as to be able to raise the arms it was essential that the fastener was not fixed to the front of the shirt. This is in line with the fasteners shown on the sculptures from the south of France (1, 2).

The Greek style cuirass had a fastener which was fixed to the shirt and hooked on to the two shoulder pieces (4).

Belts
Most belts were made of leather. Parts of belts complete with the leather have been dredged from the lake at La Tène. A belt clasp was usually in the form of a hook which fastened to a ring at the other end of the belt. Early belt clasps were roughly triangular plates, often highly decorated, with a tongue at one end which was riveted to the leather belt, and a hook at the other (6).

The middle period (250-120 B.C.) belt fasteners from La Tène are much simpler: usually a ring with a hook attachment (7). In the later period the hook was often very long and sometimes hinged (8).

65

The Celtic Shield

The Romans offer battle

The two consuls, with four new legions, advanced southwards and joined up with the four legions already in Apulia. In order to restrict Hannibal's foraging, the Romans moved right up to the river Ofanto. Hannibal used his cavalry and light-armed troops to try to deter them, but the Romans managed to establish themselves at the ford over the river. The following day part of the Roman army crossed the river and established a small camp three kilometres downstream on the south bank. Here regular conflicts took place between watering parties. Both

The shields from La Tène

Parts of three Celtic shields have been recovered from the lake at La Tène. Made of oak planks, they measure about 1·1m long and 1·2cm thick in the centre, tapering towards the sides. They have a wooden spindle-shaped boss. The centre of the boss is hollowed out to allow the hand to grasp the handle. Sometimes the handgrip has an iron bracing strip. The front of the boss is reinforced by a broad iron strip nailed to the planking of the shield.

Shields of this type have been found in Denmark and Ireland. These are hide covered. The La Tène shields must also have been covered with hide, or possibly felt. Bare wood would have split when used against slashing swords.

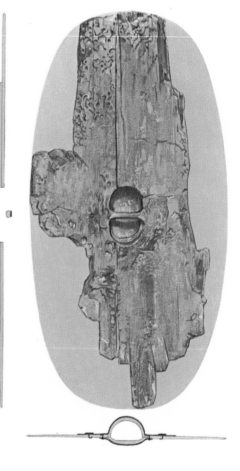

▲ Front, back and sections of one of the Celtic shields from La Tène in Switzerland. c.250 B.C., scale 1:10.

▲ Sculpture of a warrior with typical Celtic shield: from Mondragon, Vaucluse, south of France.

The origin of the Celtic shield

The origin of the shield is obscure. The similarities between the Roman and the Celtic shield are so remarkable that they must have the same origin. The earliest evidence for the Celtic shield is the Halstatt scabbard of c.400 B.C. (see p.51). The evidence for the Roman type predates this by more than two centuries.

The Celts may well have got their spined shield from the Italians but they must have used shields before coming to Italy. The Celtic style of fighting demands a shield.

The strength of the Celtic shield

Celtic shields must have been pretty strong and heavy. A shield of the La Tène type with hide covering must have weighed about 6 to 7 kg.

Shields sometimes had a metal binding. This was usually on the upper rim as a protection against chopping weapons.

When fighting in close order the Celts overlapped their shields. Caesar claims that the heavy Roman *pilum*, against which no shield was particularly effective, pierced right through the Celtic shields, pinning them together.

sides were eager for battle.

Early on the morning of August 2, 216 B.C., the Romans led their forces out of the larger camp and crossed the river. Here they were joined by the forces from the smaller camp. The legions were formed up densely in the centre, with the Roman citizen cavalry on the right and the allied cavalry on the left. Paullus commanded the right wing and Varro the left. The legions in the centre were commanded by the two consuls of the previous year, Geminus and Regulus (Flaminius' replacement).

When Hannibal saw the Roman forces drawn up he sent out his pikemen and light-armed troops as a covering force, and behind these he drew up the rest of his army. He placed his Celts and Spaniards in the middle. At the Trebbia the Romans had broken through the Carthaginian centre. Hannibal was determined that this would not happen again. So he advanced his centre to form a crescent to break the force of the Roman charge. On the right wing he placed his Numidian horsemen and on the left his Celtic and Spanish cavalry. He then withdrew his African pikemen and formed them up in column behind the cavalry at each end of the crescent.

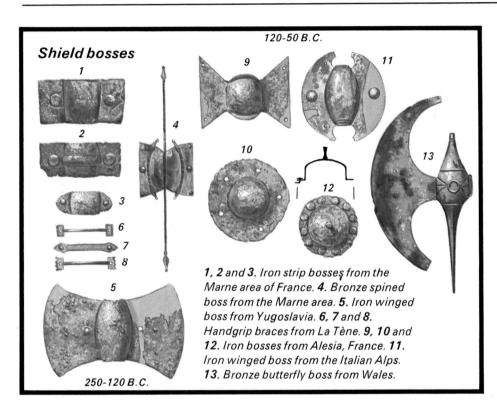

Shield bosses

120-50 B.C.

1, 2 and 3. Iron strip bosses from the Marne area of France. 4. Bronze spined boss from the Marne area. 5. Iron winged boss from Yugoslavia. 6, 7 and 8. Handgrip braces from La Tène. 9, 10 and 12. Iron bosses from Alesia, France. 11. Iron winged boss from the Italian Alps. 13. Bronze butterfly boss from Wales.

250-120 B.C.

▲ Sculpted shields from the arch at Orange in southern France, and from the Victory Frieze at Pergamon, Turkey.

Shield bosses

The series of bosses shown above trace development from the simple strip boss of the 3rd century B.C. to the elaborate butterfly boss found in Britain in the 1st century A.D. Although all the bosses except (13) were found on the continent, similar types have been found in Britain.

Shape and decoration

The majority of Celtic shields are oval but they are occasionally shown as rectangular, hexagonal, or round. Shields are decorated with symbols, animals or geometric designs. Diodorus claims that the motifs were made of bronze but they were probably painted.

The elaborate bronze shields found in Britain were for ceremonial purposes and would not have been used in battle.

▲ A mailed Celtic chief from France with his long slashing sword, and a British Celt tattooed with woad, c.50 B.C.

The Legions at Cannae

The vast Roman forces outnumbered Hannibal's by almost two to one. Hannibal had taken every possibility into account. Now was the moment of truth.

As usual the battle was begun by the light-armed and the cavalry. On the left wing the Carthaginian horsemen tore into their opponents. The Romans fought bravely, but they were no match for the Celts and Spaniards. The Romans dragged their enemies from their horses and struggled on the ground. But nothing stemmed the tide. Relentlessly the Romans were driven back along the river bank.

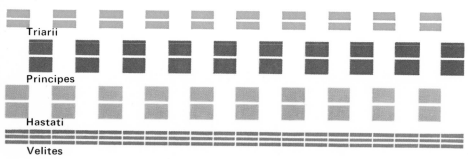

Triarii

Principes

Hastati

Velites

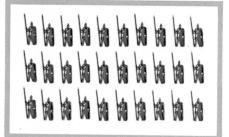

▲ The legion in battle formation with the velites *(light-armed)* drawn up in front.
◄ A maniple of triarii *(spearmen)*.
▼ A maniple of hastati *(heavy javelineers)* in standard formation. A principes maniple would be the same.

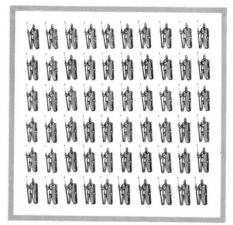

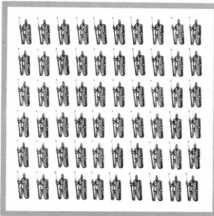

The manipular tactic

The legion still has spaces between the maniples so that the lines can interchange. This brings us to the question of how the maniples were organized. Did the *hastati* and *principes* really fight with gaps in their line, as Polybius seems to suggest, or did they close the gaps, as Livy says the *triarii* do (p.33)?

Each maniple was made up of two centuries. Polybius says the senior centurion of the maniple served on the right. But we know centurions were named front *(prior)* and back *(posterior)*. Is this a contradiction, or were the centuries lined up one behind the other with the rear century moving into the gap to form an unbroken line when battle began?

Thus the legion would form up with the *velites* in front skirmishing with the enemy. When the enemy came within range, the *velites* would be recalled and would pass through the gaps. The rear centuries of the *hastati* would close the gaps and charge (right, Phase 1).

If the *hastati* charge did not break the enemy, the recall was sounded. The *posterior* centuries would disengage and retreat until they could fall in behind the *prior* centuries. The whole line would retreat through the gaps in the *principes*, who also charged the enemy.

The new legions

Since the Latin war (340-338 B.C.), the legions had been transformed. The legion was now divided into 30 units or maniples: 10 *principes*, 10 *hastati* and 10 *triarii*. The old *rorarii* have disappeared altogether, reducing the strength of the legion from about 5,000 to 4,200. The 1,200 light-armed *accensi* and *leves*, now called *velites*, are distributed throughout the 30 maniples.

The maniples of *triarii* are still 60 strong. The *principes* and *hastati* maniples have been doubled. Each legion also had about 300 Roman cavalry, about 4,200 allied infantry, and 900 allied cavalry.

An orderly retreat

If both lines were beaten, the *hastati* would break ranks, pass through the *triarii* and re-form behind (Phase 2).

Now the *principes* would be given the order to retreat and they would reopen the gaps. Then they would withdraw through the *triarii* and into the gaps in the *hastati*. The *triarii* would now fill their gaps and present a hedge of spears to the enemy. The legion could then retreat in good order.

Both sides now withdrew their light-armed troops. The legionaries clashed their javelins against their shields. Celts, Spaniards and Romans rent the air with their war-cries. Horns, trumpets and *carnyxes* added to the raucous din. Then both sides charged. The Romans crashed into the centre of the crescent. On and on they thrust until they had flattened the formation and still they came on.

On the right wing the Numidians skirmished with their opponents trying to draw them away from the legions. On the left the way was finally clear. The Celtic and Spanish cavalry burst through. Leaving some of their number to pursue the Romans along the river-bank, the rest crossed behind the legions and descended on the rear of the allied cavalry. The Italians, seeing them coming broke and fled.

Hannibal had accomplished his masterplan. The legionaries had pushed his centre back so far that they had passed the African pikemen on either wing. All that remained was to execute the *coup de grâce*. The pikemen now faced inwards and charged the Roman flanks. The Celtic and Spanish cavalry left the Numidians to complete the destruction of the allied cavalry and attacked the legions in the rear.

The manipular tactic

Phase I

Phase II

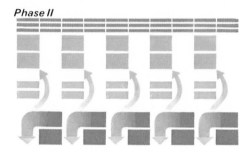

Phase III

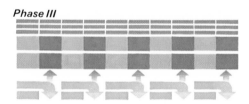

Phase I
The battle is begun by the velites. *They then retire through the gaps. The* hastati *close the gaps, and charge.*

Phase II
The rear centuries of the hastati *disengage, and reopen the gaps. The* hastati *withdraw through the* principes. *The* principes *close their gaps and charge.*

Phase III
The rear centuries of the principes *disengage and reopen the gaps. The whole line withdraws through the gaps in the* triarii. *The rear centuries of the* triarii *move up to form a solid phalanx, and the whole army retreats.*

The legions at Cannae

Polybius says that there were eight legions at Cannae. Many scholars maintain that Hannibal's 50,000 troops could not encircle an army nearly twice their size. Is this view justified?

Consular armies were usually two legions, but armies of four legions had been used against the Celts in 225 B.C. The situation in 216 B.C. can hardly have been considered less serious. The Cannae army was commanded by the two consuls and two proconsuls, which implies eight legions. Furthermore, Hannibal's formation suggests he was outnumbered.

Objectors say there were only 6,000 Roman cavalry: there should have been 10,000. But Hannibal had wiped out 4,000 after the battle of Lake Trasimeno.

The Roman battle formation

In Polybius' words the legions were drawn up so that "the depth of the maniples was many times their width". A normal century was probably six deep. If this were 'doubled' a maniple would be 24 deep and five wide. The total length of the infantry would have been 1,500m.

Polybius says cavalry may be a maximum of eight deep. In this formation, 800 cavalry had a front of 200m. Around 1,500 Roman cavalry were massed on the river bank. They would have occupied about 400m., and 4,500 allies on the left, about 1,100m. The total Roman front would have been about 3km.

Ten thousand infantry were left in camp with orders to attack Hannibal's camp during the battle. Who were they?

It had become customary to leave the *triarii* to guard the camp. The generals did not think they would need them. Previous defeats had been caused by irresponsible generals. So it is safe to assume that the 9,600 *triarii* were the "10,000" left in camp: there was no defensive rear line.

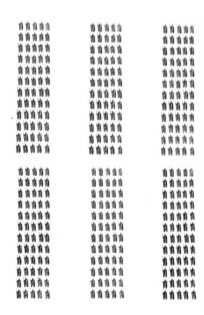

▲ *Three maniples of* hastati *and three of* principes *as they formed up at the battle of Cannae. In Polybius's words "their depth was many times their width".*

Cannae

The legions were now assailed from every side. The pressure was taken off the Celts and Spaniards who were at last able to regroup and charge. It was the bloodiest day in Roman history. Paullus was killed fighting in the ranks. Geminus and Regulus also fell. Of the legionaries, 50,000 fell where they stood, fighting to the bitter end. Ten thousand were captured: a few escaped. Hannibal had achieved the most outstanding victory of all time.

As the news spread, all the southern Italians flocked to Hannibal's banner. He marched in

The site of Hannibal's camp

The village of Cannae is on the ridge of hills at the southern end of the plain of Foggia, in Apulia. The Ofanto flows along the northern edge of the ridge.

Hannibal camped north of the river. There is only one defensible position on the north bank, the spur on which the town of San Ferdinando stands. It has steep escarpments on two sides. The Romans forced their way up to the ford just east of Hannibal's camp, stopping him foraging north of the river. Later, they established a second camp 3km downstream on the other side.

The changing course of the river

The river Ofanto has changed its course many times. The extent of the river's flooding is illustrated by the series of dykes on the north side. The 5m contour lines reveal other possible beds for the river (see map). This account is based on the belief that in Hannibal's time the river followed a more northerly course (marked **XX** on the map) leaving a plain about 2km wide to the south.

The site of the battle

The Romans chose the south side of the river. In this restricted space they hoped to be able to neutralize Hannibal's vastly superior cavalry and to decide the battle with the infantry. They lined up obliquely across the plain with their right wing resting on the river and their left on the hills.

Hannibal's forces

Hannibal had a little over 40,000 infantry and 10,000 cavalry. He had arrived in Italy with 12,000 African infantry, 8,000 Spanish infantry and 6,000 cavalry. His losses had been small, so the number of Celts can be estimated at 20,000 infantry and 4,000 cavalry. About 30 per cent of the infantry would be light-armed.

This would leave about 8,000 African pikemen, 6,000 Spanish swordsmen and 14,000 Celtic swordsmen, of whom about 4,000 probably guarded the camp. As Hannibal placed the Numidian cavalry opposite the 4,500 allied horse, the Numidians must have numbered at least 4,000, leaving 2,000 Spanish horsemen.

▲ *The battlefield at Cannae showing the old course of the river. Hannibal's camp is at the top left. The 1st Roman camp is in the middle. The 2nd Roman camp is on the right.*

▼ *A map of the battle area with 5m contours. Alternative courses for the river are in broken blue line. The Roman camps are marked **R1** and **R2**.*

-------- **Battle line** _____ **Dykes**

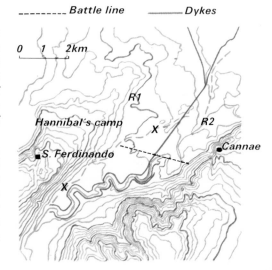

triumph across Italy. In Campania the people of Capua lined the roads and welcomed him into their city. It seemed that Hannibal had united the traditional enemies of Rome. But he could not break the Roman spirit. Every available man was called up. Even volunteer slaves and criminals were enrolled. All talk of peace was rejected. The Romans prepared to fight to the death. Before Cannae the Romans marched to battle. After Cannae they marched to war.

By 212 B.C. Rome had 25 legions in the field. They refused to fight Hannibal in open battle, but used their vast manpower to win back all the towns now on Hannibal's side. In the end, Hannibal was besieged in the toe of Italy. The legions conquered Spain and invaded Africa. Hannibal had to leave Italy to defend his homeland. He had been in Italy 15 years without a defeat. His great army had now faded away. In 202 B.C. he was defeated by Scipio, the son of his first Roman opponent.

The Romans were not magnanimous: they hounded Hannibal from country to country until finally he committed suicide. Fifty years later they launched an unprovoked attack on Carthage. They destroyed the city and sold its citizens into slavery.

The Battle: Phase I

When Hannibal saw the Romans drawn up he sent out his slingers and pikemen as a covering force. He drew up the rest of his army behind. He placed 6,000 Celtic and Spanish cavalry opposite the 1,500 Romans. On the other wing he posted his 4,000 Numidians. In the middle he drew up his 16,000 Celtic and Spanish swordsmen in alternate companies, in a crescent, deeper in the centre than the wings. He formed up the pikemen in two columns behind the cavalry.

Phase II

As usual the battle was begun by the light-armed who then withdrew to the rear. The Spanish and Celtic cavalry smashed into the Roman horsemen, driving them back along the river bank. On the other wing the Numidians skirmished with the allied cavalry, trying to draw them away from the legions. In the centre the legions crashed into the Celts and Spaniards flattening the crescent.

Phase III

When the Roman cavalry had been scattered, most of the Celts and Spaniards crossed behind the legions and charged the rear of the allied cavalry, which broke under the double assault. The legions continued to press forward until they had passed the pikemen on either wing. These now turned inwards and charged the legions in the flanks.

Phase IV

The Spanish and Celtic cavalry turned once again and charged the legions in the rear. On the wings the pikemen thrust into the Roman infantry, and extended their lines to engulf the wings further. The light-armed would now have moved round to the rear. The legions began to crumble: the pressure was taken off the Celts and Spaniards in the centre.

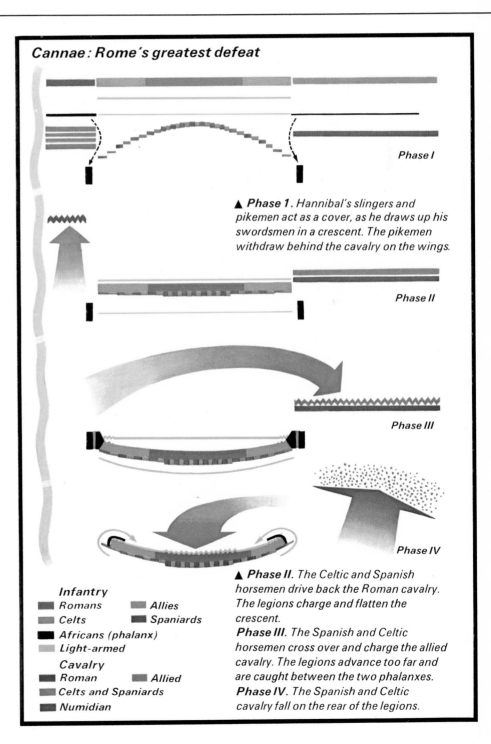

Cannae: Rome's greatest defeat

Infantry
- Romans
- Celts
- Africans (phalanx)
- Light-armed
- Allies
- Spaniards

Cavalry
- Roman
- Celts and Spaniards
- Numidian
- Allied

▲ **Phase 1**. Hannibal's slingers and pikemen act as a cover, as he draws up his swordsmen in a crescent. The pikemen withdraw behind the cavalry on the wings.

▲ **Phase II**. The Celtic and Spanish horsemen drive back the Roman cavalry. The legions charge and flatten the crescent.

Phase III. The Spanish and Celtic horsemen cross over and charge the allied cavalry. The legions advance too far and are caught between the two phalanxes.

Phase IV. The Spanish and Celtic cavalry fall on the rear of the legions.

Hannibal's Triumphal Entry into Capua

Hannibal is shown riding on the last of his elephants. He is being led by three Campanian horseman. In front of the elephant is a Celt in ceremonial armour and next to him is a Carthaginian horseman carrying the standard of Carthage.

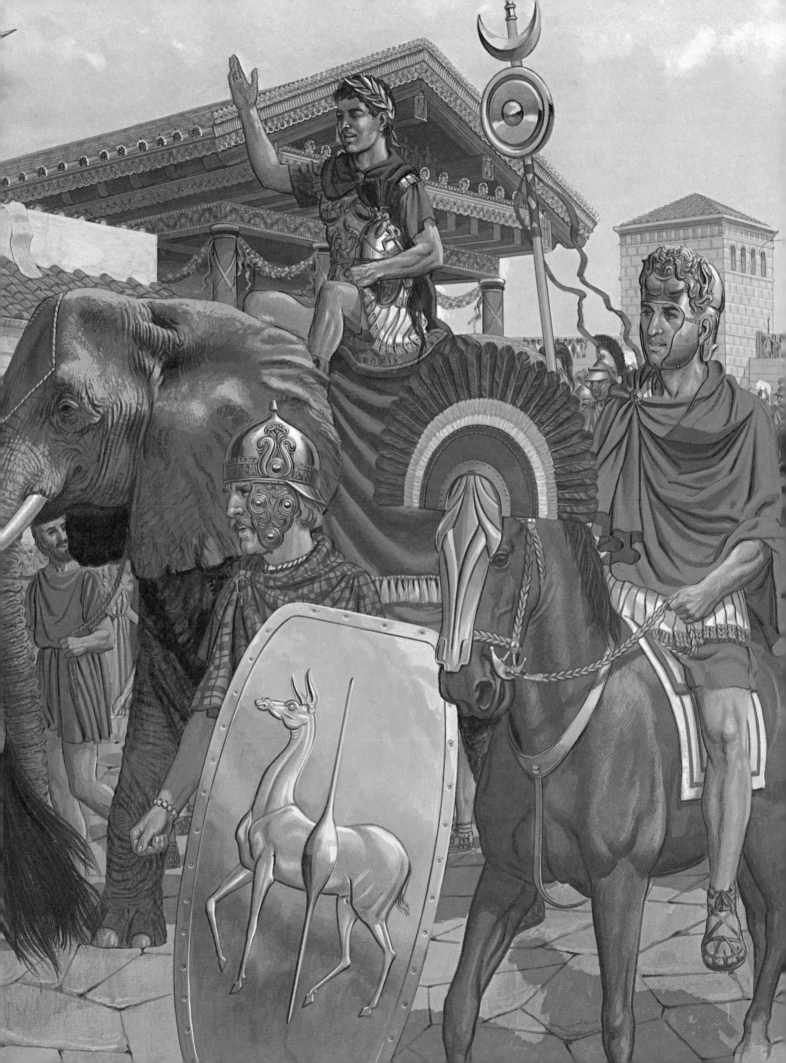

Glossary

accensi troops who, according to Livy served behind the *triarii*.

Argive shield the round shield used by Greek hoplites.

Attic helmet a helmet type which originated in Greece.

boss a domed projection. On a shield, the reinforced part covering the handgrip.

butt the foot of a spear or a javelin.

Capestrano warrior statue of a 6th-century B.C. Italian warrior discovered at the town of Capestrano in central Italy.

carnyx a Celtic trumpet.

Caudine peace the treaty forced on Rome after the capture of her army at the Caudine Forks in 321 B.C.

centurion commander of a century.

century a unit nominally of 100 men. Usually it was about 80 strong but sometimes had as few as 30 (*triarii*).

Certosa situla a bronze bucket found near Bologna in northern Italy. It was decorated with warrior figures.

chamfron face armour for a horse

chape the tip of a scabbard.

chariot a light two wheeled cart drawn by horses. It usually carried a warrior and a driver.

citadel a stronghold usually built on top of a steep-sided hill.

consul name given to each of the two chief magistrates of Rome.

cuirass armour for the torso consisting of breast and back plates usually of metal or a shirt of linen or mail.

dictator the supreme Roman magistrate, only nominated in an emergency. He was given total power usually for a period of six months.

equites the name given to the Roman upper middle class.

galley a warship propelled by oars.

gladiator a warrior who fought in the arena for the entertainment of spectators.

Gundestrup cauldron a large decorated Celtic cauldron found in Denmark.

greave leg guard.

hastati the front line of the Roman legion.

Hellenistic the name given to Greek culture and influence from c.300-c.50 B.C.

hoplite a Greek heavy armed spearman.

lamellar plates armour, made of overlapping rectangular strips of metal.

Latin League a military confederation of Latin towns in the 5th-4th centuries B.C.

legion a unit of 4-5,000 Roman troops.

leves the name given to the light-armed Roman troops in the 4th century.

liburnum a light galley.

Macedonian phalanx a type of heavy phalanx (see p.11) which was drawn up 16 or even 32 ranks deep.

mail a form of armour made of linked metal rings.

maniple the smallest operational unit of the Roman army, normally made up of two centuries.

manipular formation the formation of the Roman legion which was composed of a number of small units called maniples. These maniples could operate independently.

Montefortino helmet the commonest type of Celtic helmet. It takes its name from the ancient cemetery of the Senones at Montefortino in north-eastern Italy where several helmets were found.

Murus Gallicus a type of defensive wall built by the Celts. It was faced with stone and filled with earth laced with timber.

palisade a type of defensive fence made of wooden stakes.

panoply a complete set of armour.

pilum the heavy javelin used by Roman legionaries.

polygonal masonry irregular many-sided blocks of stone.

praetor a Roman magistrate. There were originally two elected annually. In 227 B.C. their number was increased to four. They regularly commanded armies and were subordinate only to the consuls.

principes the second line of the Roman legion.

Punic the corrupt Latin word for Phoenician.

quadrireme ancient galley with four banks of oars.

rampart a defensive wall made of earth.

Regolini-Galassi tomb a very rich 7th-century burial from southern Etruria. It contained a chariot.

rorarii troops of uncertain type who according to Livy served behind the *triarii*.

saunion a long javelin made totally of iron.

scutum the large wooden shield used by the Roman legionaries.

situla art name given to the decorated bronze buckets discovered in northern Italy and Yugoslavia.

stades measures of roughly 200 metres.

triarii the third line of the Roman legion.

velites Roman light-armed troops.

Villanovan the name given to the pre-Etruscan civilization of Italy.

woad a blue dye: Caesar described the British as decorated with woad.

People

Acrotatus son of King of Sparta. He led an expedition against Syracuse in Sicily in 314 B.C.

Alexander the Great 356–323 B.C. King of Macedon. He conquered the east as far as India.

Barca aristocratic Carthaginian family of whom Hamilcar and Hannibal were the most famous members.

Caius Terentius Varro Roman consul who commanded the allied cavalry at the Battle of Cannae.

Celts an ancient people who originated in southern Germany. During the 5th–3rd centuries B.C., they spread across the whole of western Europe and down the Danube valley. They even had a settlement in Turkey (Galatia).

Cneius Servilius Geminus Roman consul in 217 B.C. He was killed at the Battle of Cannae, 216 B.C.

Dacians a barbarian people who lived north of the river Danube.

Diodorus a Greek-Sicilian historian who lived in the first century B.C. He wrote a history of the world from the earliest times to the time of Caesar.

Dionysius of Halicarnassus a Greek historian who lived at the same time as Livy. He wrote a history of Rome from the foundation of the city up to the first war with Carthage.

Etruscans an ancient people of Italy who occupied the western coast of Italy between the river Arno and the river Tiber (Etruria).

Flaminius Roman general who defeated the Insubres at the battle of Bergamo. He was killed by Hannibal at the battle of Trasimeno 217 B.C.

Gabini the people of the ancient Latin town of Gabii, about 18km east of Rome.

Gauls The name by which the Celts of northern Italy and France were known to the Romans.

Gavius Pontius a Samnite general of exceptional ability. He was responsible for trapping the Roman army in the Caudine Forks in 321 B.C.

Hasdrubal Barca Hannibal's brother, killed by the Romans at the battle of Metaurus 207 B.C.

Hercules, Greek **Heracles**, legendary Greek hero, who may have lived c. 1,500 B.C.

Livius Titus (Livy) 59 B.C.–A.D. 17 Roman historian who wrote about Rome from its foundation to his own time.

Lucius Aemilius Paullus Roman consul, killed at the Battle of Cannae.

Liby-Phoenicians half-caste Carthaginians.

Mago Barca Hannibal's youngest brother. He came with Hannibal to Italy.

He was killed trying to get reinforcements to Africa before the battle of Zama.

Marcus Atilius Regulus Roman consul and general. He was defeated and captured by Xanthippus at the Battle of Bagradas Plains in 255 B.C. He had a son, also Marcus Atilius Regulus.

Marcus Atilius Regulus consul after the death of Flaminius in 217 B.C. He was killed in 216 B.C. at the Battle of Cannae.

Numidians the ancient nomadic peoples of Algeria/Morocco. (They made excellent light cavalry.)

Publius Cornelius Scipio father of Scipio Africanus. He failed to stop Hannibal reaching Italy, but kept him from the resources of Spain for 7 years. He and his brother were killed there in 211 B.C.

Polybius a Greek historian, died c.120 B.C. He wrote a history of the Graeco-Roman world from 220-144 B.C. He is the best ancient source for military matters.

Porsena, Lars Etruscan king of Clusium (modern Chiusi) who led the Etruscan forces against Rome after the expulsion of Tarquin the Proud.

Pyrrhus (319-272 B.C.) king of Epirus. He joined the people of Taranto and the Samnites against Rome. He defeated the Romans twice (in 280 and 279 B.C.) but failed to win the war.

Romulus the legendary founder of Rome. He is supposed to have established the city in 753 B.C.

Samnites an ancient people of Italy who occupied the mountainous country between the river Sangro and the river Ofanto (Samnium).

Scipio Africanus son of the Roman general who failed to stop Hannibal crossing Alps. Africanus defeated Hannibal at Zama in North Africa in 202 B.C. This victory earned him the name of Africanus.

Scipio family patrician family in ancient Rome, whose members made an important contribution to Rome's government and military prestige.

Sempronius Roman general who was defeated by Hannibal at the battle of the Trebbia in 218 B.C.

Senones a Celtic tribe who settled on the north eastern coast of Italy around Ancona.

Servius Tullius although of Latin origin, he became the second Etruscan king of Rome. He reorganized the Roman army c.550 B.C.

Strabo (63 B.C.- A.D. 21) a Greek geographer who wrote on the ancient world.

Tarquin the Proud the last king of Rome at the end of the 6th century B.C.

Trajan Roman emperor from A.D. 98-117.

Volsci one of the hill tribes who invaded Latium in the 5th century B.C.

Xanthippus a Spartan officer who trained the Carthaginian army and enabled them to defeat the Romans in 255 B.C.

Places and Battles

Alalia an Etruscan colony in Corsica.

Allia the site of Rome's great defeat by the Celts (390 B.C.) It is a stream running into the Tiber about 18km north of Rome.

Appian Way the coast road leading from Rome to Campania.

Apulia the area of Italy bordering Samnium to the east.

Caere (modern **Cerveteri**) an ancient town of southern Etruria.

Campania the area of Italy around the bay of Naples, bordering Samnium on the west.

Cannae the site of Rome's greatest defeat in 216 B.C.

Capua originally an Etruscan colony in Campania. It was captured by the Samnites in the 5th century B.C., became an ally of the Romans in the 4th century and went over to Hannibal's side in 216 B.C. The Romans recaptured it in 211 and a Roman colony was established there.

Carthage a Phoenician colony on the north African coast near Tunis. In the 4th-3rd centuries B.C. it became the most powerful city in the western Mediterranean.

Caudine Forks a pass through the foothills of the Apennine mountains south-east of Capua.

Clusium (modern **Chiusi**) a town of northern Etruria.

Corsica large island off the west coast of Italy.

Cumae a Greek colony just north of Naples.

Drac, river tributary of the Isère.

Durance, river, the most southerly tributary of the river Rhône.

Entremont the site of a Celtic fortress just north of Aix-en-Provence in southern France.

Epirus ancient name for north-west Greece.

Fregellae a Roman colony established on the eastern side of the Liris river.

Heraclea Pyrrhus' first victory over the Romans (280 B.C.)

Illyria the name given to the ancient country that roughly corresponds with Yugoslavia.

Isère, river, a tributary of the Rhône in southern France.

Island, the large tract of land between the Rhône and another river which Polybius calls the Skaras (probably the Isère).

Latium the area of west coast of Italy south of the river Tiber.

Lilybaeum (modern **Marsala**) town on the westernmost tip of Sicily. It was originally Carthaginian. Captured by the Romans during first war with Carthage.

Liris the river in central Italy along which the Romans and Samnites first came into contact.

Lucania the area of Italy bordering Samnium to the south.

Marseilles (ancient **Massilia**) a Greek colony on the south coast of France. It was an ally of Rome at the time of Hannibal.

Milan ancient capital of the Insubres in northern Italy.

Naples (ancient **Neapolis**) a Greek colony on the west coast of Italy.

Narce a town in Etruria. A fine Villanovan helmet and cuirass were found there.

Ofanto (ancient **Aufidus**) the river that marked the southern border of Samnium.

Palatine hill a hill at Rome where the original town was founded in the 8th century B.C.

Pergamon a Hellenistic city in Asia Minor (modern Turkey).

Phoenicia the homeland of the Phoenicians roughly corresponding to modern Lebanon.

Pompeii ancient town in the bay of Naples. It was destroyed when the volcano Vesuvius erupted in A.D. 79.

Battle of Pydna Roman victory over the Macedonians, 168 B.C. The Roman commander was Aemilius Paullus, son of the general killed by Hannibal at Cannae.

Sicily large island off the south-west coast of Italy. It was colonized by the Greeks and Carthaginians.

Sorrento (ancient **Surrentum**) a town at the southern end of the bay of Naples.

Sparta a town in southern Greece famous for its military traditions.

Tarquinii (modern **Tarquinia**) an ancient town of southern Etruria.

Telamon site in Etruria of the defeat of the Celts by the Romans in 225 B.C.

La Tène a village on the north side of Lake Neuchâtel in Switzerland. The site was used by the Celts for the dedication of the spoils of war. Hundreds of weapons have been dredged from the lake here.

Tiber the river on which Rome was built. It formed the southern and eastern borders of Etruria.

Trasimeno, Lake a lake in Etruria where the Romans were defeated by Hannibal in 217 B.C.

Trebbia, river, a tributary of the Po: the Romans were defeated by Hannibal here in 218 B.C.

Tuscany modern name for Etruria. It only roughly corresponds to the ancient area.

Veii an ancient Etruscan town only 14 km north of Rome. It is famous for the 10-year Roman siege which ended with the fall of the town in 396 B.C.

Vetulonia an ancient town of central Etruria.

Volsinii an ancient town in southern Etruria.

Vulci an ancient town in southern Etruria.

Index